English

Contents

3

Education First
EF

Unit 5

Dealing with disaster

Disasters and accidents:
Emergency preparations and extreme weather

Family values

Families:
Families, children's games and nursery rhymes

Unit 7

Good behaviour

Manners and behaviour:
Cultural stereotypes and culture shock

Looking back, moving forward

Revision:
Reading skills and different text types, customs around the world

Focus

Functions

Dealing with disaster	Family values	Good behaviour	Looking back, moving forward
Talking about disasters and emergencies	Talking about families	Talking about manners and good behaviour	Improving reading skills
Identifying and describing extreme weather conditions	Describing games	Describing cultural stereotypes	Presenting a grammar lesson
Making preparations	Saying nursery rhymes	Making a presentation	Identifying and describing different text types
	Talking about how things used to be		Comparing customs around the world

---

Skills

Dealing with disaster	Family values	Good behaviour	Looking back, moving forward
Reading: Reading an article about earthquakes. Reading information about hurricanes	**Reading:** Reading descriptions of games. Reading an article about 'latchkey kids'	**Reading:** Reading about cultural conventions. Reading about culture shock	**Reading:** Speed reading skills. Reading about Latin America
Writing: Writing a news article. Writing a disaster plan	**Writing:** Writing a description of a game	**Writing:** Writing a report on taboos. Writing polite emails	**Writing:** Identifying different text types. Writing different text types
Listening: Listening to advice on disasters. Listening to witness accounts	**Listening:** Listening to a discussion about ageing. Listening for rhyming words	**Listening:** Listening to a radio show	**Listening:** Listening to a conversation about work. Listening to questions
Speaking: Giving a presentation. Interviewing an eyewitness	**Speaking:** Describing family. Comparing now and then	**Speaking:** Describing culture shock. Interviewing people	**Speaking:** Asking about cultural differences. Giving a presentation about work

---

Grammar

Dealing with disaster	Family values	Good behaviour	Looking back, moving forward
Conjunctions of time	Using 'used to'	Adjective + infinitive combinations	Defining and non-defining relative clauses
Passive and active voice		Using 'used to'	Question forms
Quantifiers			

Vocabulary / Pronunciation

Dealing with disaster	Family values	Good behaviour	Looking back, moving forward
Extreme weather conditions	Families and family members	Cultural stereotypes	Question words
Use of 'the' with geographical features	Giving advice	Culture shock	Work-related vocabulary
Hurricane and earthquake vocabulary	Rhyming words	Taboos	Reading skills
	Pronouncing 'used to'	Email etiquette	Past tense verb endings
	Pronouncing past tense endings	Email acronyms	Identifying specific sounds

# of life

After this unit, you should be able to ...

- Use vocabulary related to food
- Read and write recipes
- Use adjectives to make comparisons
- Compare adverbs
- Use determiners
- Compare life in different countries
- Use intonation correctly

A Stand up and talk to your classmates. Find someone who ...

- has eaten something really strange
- never eats breakfast
- prefers food from a country that is not their home country
- is good at cooking
- has lived in more than two countries
- thinks Mexican food is tastier than French food
- thinks Japanese food is more delicious than Italian food
- has eaten food from more than eight different countries
- has never eaten at McDonald's
- has travelled to more than five countries

B Now get into pairs and tell your partner about some of the people you spoke to.

C Still in pairs, choose two countries from the following list and brainstorm some adjectives which describe life, people and food in both places.

Mexico	The United Kingdom
Australia	France
Russia	Thailand
The United States	Canada
Italy	Brazil
New Zealand	China

D Now write some sentences comparing the two countries you have chosen.

■ EXAMPLE

Food in China is oilier than food in Australia.

Vocabulary and Grammar

A Answer these questions.

1 What does your best friend <u>like</u>? *Hobbies, interests, sports, etc*
_____

2 What <u>is</u> your best friend like? *Personality*
_____

3 What does your best friend <u>look like</u>? *Physically*
_____

- What is the difference in meaning between these three questions?
- What kind of information is the speaker looking for?
- What is the verb in each question?

B Read this description and answer the questions.

My best friend, Bob, is cheerful and warm-hearted. He isn't especially outgoing, but he is considerate and attentive. I tell people he is like a teddy bear. Bob has shoulder-length, wavy blonde hair. He has warm brown eyes. He is fairly tall. He is a bit heavier than he should be. He doesn't work out at the gym, so he looks like a marshmallow.

1 Which two questions from Exercise A does this description answer?
2 & 3
_____

2 What verbs are used the most?
is, has
_____

3 Notice that even though the word 'like' is in the question, it is not always in the answer. When do we use the word 'like'?
When we want more information about someone/thing, in questions.

4 What kind of word comes after 'like'?
article
_____
_____

5 Do we use 'like' before an adjective?
_____

C Write a description of a family member or someone else close to you. Remember to include a physical description, a description of their personality and to say what they like to do. Share your description with the class.

D Read the descriptions below and guess which foods are being described.

1 *Ice Cream* It is smooth, creamy and very cold. It tastes very sweet.
2 *Lemon* It's yellow, and it looks a bit like a tennis ball. The outside feels smooth. The inside tastes very sour. The juice is good on fish.
3 _____ It can be crunchy or smooth. It tastes great on toast or in sandwiches. People either think it smells delicious or awful.
4 *olives* They are small and black or green. They look oval or round in shape. They taste salty and can be quite oily. You can slice them up and put them on pizza.
5 *Chilis* They can be red, black or green. They taste spicy. The tiny ones are usually the hottest.
6 _____ You put this on salad. It is oily and smells like garlic. It tastes like vinegar.

Have you tried all of these kinds of food? Do you like them? Why or why not?

E Write the adjectives below under the correct heading. Some words may go under more than one heading.

round   flat   spicy   bitter   delicious   cube-shaped   bland
powdery   crumbly   disgusting   cylindrical   chewy   hard
crisp   rectangular   enormous   soft   juicy   sticky   dry
moist   mushy   garlicky   terrible   shiny   circular

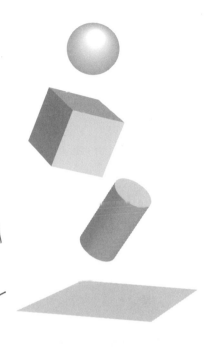

~~terrible~~ Taste	~~terrible~~ Smell	~~terrible~~ Texture	Appearance
spicy	disgusting	powdery	round
bitter	garlicky	crumbly	flat hard
garlicky delicious		chewy	cube-shaped
bland		hard	cylindrical
disgusting		crisp moist	rectangular
juicy		soft mushy	enormous
dry moist		sticky	shiny
		juicy sticky	circular

F Look again at Exercise E. What verb do we use in our description of each category?

—■ EXAMPLE —
It tastes very sweet.

taste, smell, feel, look
_____
_____

G Look back at the questions used to ask about your best friend. What questions could you make to ask about the taste, smell, texture and appearance of food? Work with a partner. Then, as a class, put the questions on the board.

Note: We can also ask: How does it taste / smell / look / feel? We answer this question in exactly the same way.

—■ EXAMPLE —
What does it taste like?

H Look at these two examples from the food descriptions in Exercise D.

—■ EXAMPLES —
They taste spicy.
It tastes like vinegar.

Complete this rule:
We don't use 'like' before a / an _____.
We only use 'like' before a / an _____.
Be careful! It is true that 'taste' and the other words are used as nouns. However, we do not usually say 'The taste is spicy' or 'Its taste is spicy'.

I For the next lesson, bring in some food for the class to try. Your teacher will explain what kinds of food would be good.

Speaking and Vocabulary

A *'There's no accounting for taste.'*

Discussion beginning

This is a popular quotation in English. What do you think it means? Discuss with a partner, and then share your ideas with the class.

B Your teacher will help you set up for your taste test. Work in groups. Your teacher will assign you a food to try. In your group, discuss the taste, smell, texture and appearance of your food. Use the vocabulary on page 3 to help you make your notes, then fill in the first row of the chart below.

Project

Food	Taste	Smell	Texture	Appearance
1				
2				
3				
4				
5				
6				

C Next, you are going to interview people who tried the other foods. Your teacher will tell you who to interview. Ask about the taste, smell, texture and appearance of his or her food and fill in the other rows of your chart.

> **■ EXAMPLE**
> *What does X taste like?*
> *It tastes salty.*

When you are finished, try the other kinds of food. Which is your favourite? Why? Take a class poll. What did people like the most? What was the least favourite?

D Write a description of your favourite food (in real life, not from the taste test). Imagine you are describing it to someone who has never seen or tasted it before, and you want him or her to understand exactly why you love it.

_____
_____
_____
_____
_____
_____

E Can you match the following traditional dishes to their country of origin?

1	dim sum	H	☐ a France
2	lasagne	i	☐ b Thailand
3	roast beef and Yorkshire pudding	f	c Mexico
4	sashimi	J	d Spain
5	gai massaman	☐	e Japan
6	pozole	D	f England
7	tapas	C	☐ g Morocco
8	vichyssoise	☐	h China
9	couscous	☐	i Italy

F Look at these cooking verbs. Do you know what they mean? Take turns ~~miming them to the~~ *describing them, follow w/*
~~class.~~ If you know any other cooking verbs, share them with your classmates. *1 example*

e.g. To cook rice, first you must mix oil + rice...

cut	slice	chop	dice	grate	sift	pour
mix	stir	beat	melt	boil	fry	bake

G Now look at these abbreviations. Write the full version of each measurement.
The first example has been done for you. Then read about measurements.

1 lb ___pound___
2 oz _ounce_
3 pt _pint_
4 qt _quart_
5 tbsp _tablespoon_
6 tsp _teaspoon_
7 °C _Celcius_
8 °F _fahrenheit_
9 kg _kilograms_
10 g _grams_
11 l _litres_
12 ml _millilitres_

Most countries in the world use a system of measurement called 'metric'. The metric system is fairly simple to understand. Most measurements are broken down into groups of one thousand, one hundred or ten. For example: to measure height, we use metres. One metre is one hundred centimetres. One centimetre is ten millimetres. To measure the volume of a liquid, we use litres. One litre is one thousand millilitres.

In the United Kingdom and some other countries, an older, more complicated system of measurement called 'imperial' is also used. For example, the imperial system measures weight using pounds and ounces. One pound contains 16 ounces.

In recipes, you will often see the measurement word 'cup', e.g. 'three cups of flour'. This does not mean the same thing as a cup that you drink from. One cup is around 250 ml (1/4 litre), although this amount changes slightly from country to country.

H Look at the list of abbreviated measurements again. Mark an 'M' next to the metric measurements and an 'I' next to the imperial measurements.

1 lb M   2 oz ___   3 pt ___   4 qt ___   5 tbsp ___   6 tsp ___
7 °C ___   8 °F ___   9 kg ___   10 g ___   11 l ___   12 ml ___

I Now place the measurements in the table below, according to what they measure.
Think about recipes you have read. Write down some of the things each type of unit
is used to measure. The first example has been done for you.

Weight	Volume of a liquid	Temperature
grammes (dry goods, flour, butter, sugar, meat, cheese)		

Listening and Writing

A Listen to this episode of the TV cooking show, *The Well-Dressed Chef*. The first time you listen, decide what the chef is making. Also, circle the ingredients he uses.

Name of dish:

_____

_____ butter	_____ oil
_____ flour	_____ ground cloves
_____ milk	_____ sugar
_____ eggs	_____ nuts
_____ brown sugar	_____ ginger ale
_____ raisins	_____ vanilla
_____ baking soda	_____ cinnamon
_____ oats	_____ nutmeg
_____ potato chips	_____ chocolate chips

B Listen again to the first part. How much of each ingredient does he use? Make a note in front of each ingredient.

C Listen to the second part again and put the instructions in order.

___ Add the eggs and vanilla, and beat.
___ Stir in the oats, raisins and chocolate chips.
___ Beat together the butter and the brown sugar.
___ Pre-heat the oven to 180 degrees Celsius.
___ Drop heaped tablespoons of the cookie mixture onto the baking sheets.
___ Add this to the butter mixture, and mix.
___ Bake them for 10–12 minutes.
___ Sift the flour, baking soda, cinnamon and cloves.

D Read this recipe. How is it organised? When you give instructions, what verb form do you use?

Beef Wellington

Ingredients: 1 2lb piece of fillet steak
1 sheet of puff pastry dough
1 chopped onion   1 chopped leek
1 clove of garlic, crushed
6 oz of pâté   1 egg
2 tbsp butter   2 tbsp oil

Method:
1   Pre-heat the oven to 200°C.
2   Sprinkle the fillet with salt and pepper.
3   Melt the butter and oil together in a large saucepan.
4   Fry the onion, garlic and leek for a few minutes.
5   Add the pâté. Add salt and pepper and allow the ingredients to cool.
6   Roll out the puff pastry until it is thin.
7   Place some of the pâté mixture in the centre of the pastry and place the piece of fillet steak on top.
8   Fold the pastry over the fillet to form a package and brush with a little beaten egg.
9   Place the package on a greased baking tray.
10 Place in the oven for 15 minutes for a rare fillet, 25 minutes if you want it well done.

E Choose your favourite dish, or a national dish from your country. First, list the ingredients you will need. How much of each ingredient do you need to have?

Name of dish: _____
Ingredients: _____
_____

F Write the steps you need to follow.

Grammar and Vocabulary

A Your teacher will give you a card with a word on it. Don't show anyone your word. Make sure you know what the word means. Then say, 'How are you, today?' in the way that the card tells you to. Your classmates will try to guess your word.

B What type of word did you get in Exercise A? What are these words used for? What is the most common ending for these words?

_____
_____
_____
_____
_____

C Complete the rules.

Adverbs of manner describe or modify _____, _____ and other _____. They are most often formed by adding _____ to an adjective. They answer the question _____.

D Read these sentence pairs. What is the difference in meaning between the adverbs?

My father works *hard*. He comes home exhausted.
My brother is lazy. He *hardly* works.

I apologised because I arrived *late* to the meeting.
Have you read any good books *lately*?

Nancy makes me nervous because she always drives too *near* the centre of the road.
Last week, we *nearly* had an accident because of it.

Have you ever seen a belly flop? It's when a person dives into a pool and falls *flat* on their stomach.
My teacher *flatly* refused to let me miss class to watch the football final.

E What other irregular adverbs do you know? Write them in the boxes below.

Adjective	Adverb	Note
		Be careful! These words end in '-ly', but they are adjectives, not adverbs: lovely, friendly, silly, lonely, early (both an adjective and adverb).

Grammar and Vocabulary

F We can use adverbs with adjectives to give more information about something.

> ■ **EXAMPLE**
> *This soufflé is extremely light and delicately seasoned.*

We know how light it is and how much it is seasoned.
Notice that you could replace 'extremely' with an adverb of degree, such as 'very', 'really' or 'quite'. However, we often use certain adverbs of manner to intensify the adjective. Do you know any other words which can be used this way?

H Work with a partner. Make five sentences, using one word from the left column and one from the right. Remember that you need to change the words in the left column into adverbs! (Be careful! A few combinations do not collocate.)

> ■ **EXAMPLE**
> *The food at that restaurant was absolutely disgusting.*

terrible		talented
extreme		sorry
true		polite
unusual		delicious
awful		intelligent
absolute		disgusting
remarkable		
surprising		

G What do you think the sentence below means? Based on this information, would you eat at the restaurant, or not?

> ■ **EXAMPLE**
> *The food at the new restaurant is awfully delicious.*

I Using the adverbs you have learned, write a few sentences about a meal you have eaten recently. You can write about a good meal or a bad meal.

> ■ **EXAMPLE**
> *I ate an unusually delicious meal at my local café last week.*

Reading and Writing

A You are going to read a restaurant review. What information do you expect to read in a review of a restaurant?

Read the review. Is it mostly positive, or mostly negative? What kind of restaurant is it?
Do you think you would go to this restaurant? Why or why not? ~~Share your ideas with a partner~~.

The Village Club

From the moment you walk in through the door, everything about the Village Club says 'class'. From the beautifully dressed, helpful waiters in their white jackets and gloves, to the lovely violin background music, attention is paid to every detail. The Village Club is about more than just fine food.

I was meeting a friend there, so we decided to have cocktails in the comfortable bar before dinner. The expertly mixed cosmopolitans had just the right balance of sweet cranberry juice and a sharp taste of lime. From the bar, we could look into both the tea room and the main dining room. The tea room was bright and cheerful. Colourfully-patterned comfy chairs were crowded around small low tables, which were covered in flowers. The rose-scented air drifted out towards us whenever guests left. I imagined falling asleep in the warm room, and I was glad we would be eating in the main dining room. The elegant Victorian design in that room was tasteful and understated. A few circular tables stood along each wall of the candlelit room. Sturdy, high-backed chairs with soft cushions surrounded the tables. The room smelled like leather and oak, and the aroma of a perfectly cooked steak made my mouth water. As I sipped my drink, diners' forks and knives clinked softly, and their quiet conversations provided a soothing background to our dining experience.

The menu was unusually extensive, including appetisers such as spinach and ricotta ravioli, main dishes like juicy steak served with fresh vegetables, and dangerously rich-sounding desserts, such as the double chocolate cake with bitter chocolate cream.

I decided on a simple salad to start with, while my friend went for the tomato and basil soup. For main course we chose the fillet of veal parmesan and the baked salmon. My salad was extremely fresh with a deliciously tart dressing. On the other hand, my friend thought the soup tasted a little salty. The veal was extremely tender. The sauce tasted a bit garlicky, but it was not overpowering, and the perfectly melted cheese complemented it. Unfortunately, while the salmon smelled wonderful, it was overcooked and a bit dry, and the vegetables were bland.

After this, we were too full for dessert, so that will have to wait for next time, and, for me, there certainly will be a next time.

The Village Club is at 23 George Street, Birmingham.
Open for dinner 5–10 pm, Tuesday–Sunday,
closed Monday. Prices start at £25 per person.

B Are there any words in the reading you don't understand? Use a dictionary to check their meaning.

C Match each word to its meaning.

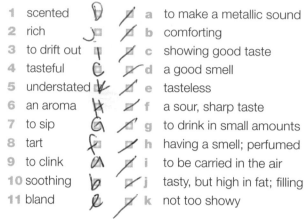

1 scented
2 rich
3 to drift out
4 tasteful
5 understated
6 an aroma
7 to sip
8 tart
9 to clink
10 soothing
11 bland

a to make a metallic sound
b comforting
c showing good taste
d a good smell
e tasteless
f a sour, sharp taste
g to drink in small amounts
h having a smell; perfumed
i to be carried in the air
j tasty, but high in fat; filling
k not too showy

D Underline the adjectives and circle the adverbs in Exercise A on page 9. How many adverb-adjective combinations can you find? After the verbs 'taste' and 'smell', were there adjectives or adverbs? Why?

E Look again at the second paragraph of Exercise A on page 9. It is a description of two rooms— the tea room and the main dining room. Which room would you prefer? Why?

What mood does the writer create for each room? How? Which senses does the writer use to describe the rooms? Give examples. How does using a variety of senses make the description more interesting?

F You are going to write a review of your favourite restaurant. You will need to describe the place and the atmosphere, the service and the food. In particular, you should describe one dish in detail.

First, tell your partner about the restaurant. Make sure you talk about the topics above. Be sure to use all of your senses!
When you are listening, ask questions to get more details. Try to picture the place and taste the food in your mind.

G Next, make an outline. Write some notes below.

H Now, write your review. Remember to include the name of the restaurant, the type of food they serve, the location, the average cost and the hours of operation. (If you don't know, use your language skills to find out.)

When you are finished, re-read your review. Did you use more than one of your senses? Did you use adverb and adjective combinations? Do all of your sentences have a subject and a verb? Did you remember to use full-stops between your sentences?

Listing and Speaking

A Work with a partner. Write the opposites of the adjectives in the box below. What nouns could these pairs of adjectives be used with?

Adjectives		Nouns
1 severe	light	rain, weather
2 polluted	clean	cities
3 ugly	pretty	clothes
4 cheerful	sad	people
5 cheap	expensive	stores
6 light	dark	day
7 modern	old	cities, clothes
8 casual	formal	parties
9 outgoing	shy	people
10 fresh	dirty	people, food
11 well-dressed	casual	people

B You are going to listen to part of a talk show comparing life in Japan and Mexico. What do you know about these countries? With a partner, share your ideas about the food, the climate, the people and the cost of living of the two countries.

C Listen and answer the questions.

1 Who is Fernando Lopez? Chef
2 Why was he in Japan? How long was he there?
3 What Japanese dish did he especially like?
4 How did he describe the dish?
5 What surprised him the most?
6 What really impressed Fernando?

D Listen again and take notes, filling in the chart.

	Japan	Mexico
Food		
People		
Cost of Living		
Other		

E Use your notes to complete these sentences. Then listen again and check.

1 The Japanese eat _much more_ fish _than_ Mexicans.
2 Japanese food is _much lighter_ than Mexican food. Mexican food is _not as_ light.
3 In general, Mexican food is _much spicier_ than Japanese food.
4 In Mexico, the coast is _hotter_ and _more humid_ than in the centre. In the mountains, it's _drier_ and _a bit_ cooler.
5 The winters in Japan are _quite a bit_ colder than in Mexico. They definitely have _a lot more_ snow!
6 The summers in Japan are _not as_ hot _as_ they are in Mexico.
7 The people in Japan behave quite a bit _more formally_ when they meet you. Mexicans, on the other hand, behave _more casually_.
8 The Hikari train stops _a bit more frequently_ than the fastest train. It is a _little_ slower, but it is a lot cheaper.
9 Daily life is _a bit less_ expensive in Mexico.

---

competition, 3 months
eel sushi
fresh, mild, doesn't taste like fish

5. People
6. clean & beautiful country
mix of old & new

Listening and Speaking

F What words do we use to make comparisons? Look at the sentences in Exercise E, and make rules about how to make comparisons with adjectives, adverbs and nouns. Check your answers as a class.

G Look again at the sentences in Exercise E. Complete the answers below.

Words and phrases that mean a big difference:

_____

_____

Words and phrases that mean a small difference:

_____

_____

H What is life like in your country? First, make notes about the food, the climate, the people and the way of life. Then, interview a partner. Ask your partner questions to find out about life in his or her country / hometown. Remember to form the questions correctly! Take notes on what your partner tells you.

> ■ **EXAMPLE**
> *What's the food like in Canada?*

I Now, using the notes you took about your partner's country / hometown, compare that country to the one you are in now. Present your findings to the class.

J Read the following text. Which city would you prefer to live in? Why?

London and New York are both very popular tourist destinations for visitors from all over the world. People visit these places for their theatres, museums and art galleries, and their shops.

New York is a bit bigger than London, and it has a population of more than eight million people. The climate in New York is also more extreme than in London. In winter, New York is much colder, and it is a lot warmer in summer.

Both cities have three major airports. London's largest airport, Heathrow, is a little busier than New York's JFK. However, JFK is a lot closer to the city centre than Heathrow.

Traffic is a problem in both cities. In London, cars have to drive a bit more slowly than in New York because it is a little more congested. In New York, it is much easier to find taxis because they are painted bright yellow, whereas in London, they are painted black.

Homework

You are planning to move to one of two cities. You need to compare them to decide which city will be better for you. Use the Internet to gather information about the two cities. For example, you may want information about the climate, the cost of housing, the crime rate, the environment (like pollution) and entertainment. Use your own ideas as well. Take notes. Then, for each category, write sentences comparing the two cities. Finally, choose which city you prefer, giving reasons for your decision.

Pronunciation

A In this unit, you have used different kinds of questions. We use different intonation patterns for different kinds of questions. Sometimes we use a rising tone, sometimes we use a falling tone and sometimes we use a combination.

Listen to the following questions. First, underline the stressed words. Then, mark each part of the question with a rising or falling arrow to show the intonation.

1 What sports do you like best?

2 What is your best friend like?

3 What's the weather like in England?

4 What does pizza taste like?

5 What do olives look like?

6 Are you from Korea?

7 Do you like chocolate?

8 Can I pay cash?

9 Which do you like better, football or baseball?

10 Which city do you prefer, New York or London?

11 Do you prefer Italian food or Chinese food?

12 Does this bus go to the museum or to the library?

13 Do you prefer paying by cash?

14 How would you like to pay?

B What patterns did you notice? Circle the correct word to make some rules.

1 When we ask simple questions that begin with a question word, we use rising / falling intonation.

2 When we ask simple questions without a question word, we use rising / falling intonation.

3 When we ask about a choice, our voice rises / falls on the first choice and rises / falls on the second choice.

C Work with a partner. Take turns asking and answering questions. Concentrate on using the correct intonation. Use the following prompts.

┌─■ EXAMPLES ────────────────────┐
Do you prefer football or baseball?

Which kind of food do you prefer, Italian or Chinese?
└────────────────────────────────┘

• shopping in supermarkets or in small shops?

• watching films on TV or DVD?

• listening to music on CD or MP3?

• paying by cash or by credit card?

• holidays by the sea or in the mountains?

• travelling on your own or in a group?

• receiving letters or emails?

• chocolate ice-cream or vanilla ice-cream?

• spicy food or mild food?

• formal clothes or casual clothes?

D Now make up your own questions. Use the adjectives and topics you have learnt about in this lesson.

Language Practice

A Some of these sentences are incorrect. Which ones? Correct them. There may be more than one error in the sentence.

1 I just ate raisins. Now my hand feel~~s~~ *s or S* sticky.
_____

2 He looks like a film star. _____

3 The cake's taste is delicious! *The cake tastes delicious*

4 How is he like? *What is he like*

5 ~~Its~~ *The* smell is disgusting. _____

6 She looks like happy. _____

7 He looks intelligent. _____

8 It tastes ~~like~~ sweet~~y~~. _____

9 What she does look like? _____

10 Your hand feels ~~to be~~ cold. _____

B Make questions using the words below.

> **EXAMPLE**
> lasagne / taste
> *What does lasagne taste like?*

1 durian / smell
What does durian smell like?

2 ice-cream / taste
What does ice-cream taste like?

3 your teacher / look
What does your teacher look like?

4 your home town / be
What is your home town like?

5 chicken yakitori / taste
What does chicken yakitori taste like?

6 do / your best friend / like
What does your best friend like?

7 be / your best friend / like
What is your best friend like?

C Now answer the questions in Exercise B. If you don't know the answer, ask someone else.

> **EXAMPLE**
> *Lasagne is delicious. It tastes a little garlicky.*

1 _____
2 _____
3 _____
4 _____
5 _____
6 _____
7 _____

D Fill the gaps with the correct adverb.

> hard hardly flat flatly near nearly late lately

1 You don't need an umbrella. It's _____ raining.
2 The instructions on this sweater say it has to lie _____ to dry.
3 Be careful! You _____ hit me on the head!
4 I haven't seen any good movies _____.
5 Please sit _____ the front of the room.
6 My favourite player really kicks the ball _____.
7 The train is going to get into the station _____.
8 The defendant _____ denied doing anything wrong.

E Try to fill the gaps in the sentences below with one of the adjectives from this unit.
Answers will vary.

1 Jane has a really *remarkable* personality; she is the life and soul of any party.

2 When you go to the market in France, you'll notice that the vegetables are really *delicious juicy*, like they have just been picked!

3 Chris took me to a really *expensive* restaurant. I nearly had a heart attack when the bill arrived!

4 This curry is really spicy. I prefer something a bit more *bland*.

5 Shanghai is a really *tough* city, although some areas are still very *nice*.

6 Why don't you buy some new shoes? Those are getting a little *old*.

7 What is the dress code for the party next week? Is it *conservative* or *dressy*?

8 I don't think you could describe grey as a *cheerful* colour. It's a bit depressing.

F Make sentences using comparatives, adverbs or nouns.

*** means there is a big difference
* means there is a small difference
= means there is no difference

```
───■ EXAMPLES ──────────────────────
*** Siberia / Italy / cold
Siberia is much colder than Italy.
=  Siberia / Alaska / cold
Siberia is as cold as Alaska.
────────────────────────────────────
```

1 *** Hong Kong / Sydney / skyscrapers

Hong Kong has many more skyscrapers than Sydney.

2 = living in Tokyo / living in Moscow / expensive

Living in Tokyo is as expensive as living in Moscow.

3 * Mexican food / Thai food / spicy

Mexican food is spicier than Thai food.

4 *** Russia / Brazil / snow in winter

Russia has much more snow in the winter than Brazil has

5 * the English rugby team / the French rugby team / play well

The English rugby team plays better than the French rugby team

6 * Berlin / Prague / historic buildings

Berlin has more historic buildings than Prague

7 *** angry people / calm people / speak loudly and quickly

Angry people speak much more loudly + quickly than calm people

8 = computers in Hong Kong / computers in Shanghai / cheap

Computers in Hong Kong are as cheap as computers in Shanghai.

9 *** French cheese / British cheese / smelly

French cheese is much more smelly than British cheese.

10 * lemons / olives / bitter

Lemons are more bitter than olives.

G Now write some more comparative sentences of your own.

_____

_____

_____

H Think of a festival in your country. Make notes under the following headings.

Time of year	Reason for the festival
May 5th	Cinco de Mayo, indep
Sights	Food / Tastes
Sounds	Smells

Project

I You have been asked to write an entry for a guide to festivals around the world. Write an entry of about 150 words describing a festival which you celebrate in your country. Use your notes from Exercise H. Remember to talk about all the senses in your description.

Language Reference

DESCRIPTIONS

When we ask for a description of someone or something, we can use: 'what' + to be + 'like'?

What is your new car like?

What's is the weather like in spring?

What's Chinese food like?

We usually don't use the word 'like' in the answer, unless we are comparing two things.

The weather is warm and dry.

The weather in spring here is like summer in your country.

We can use the same structure to find out more details about taste, smell, texture and appearance. We use the verb 'taste', 'smell', 'feel' and 'look'.

You can answer these questions in a variety of ways. If you use an adjective, the word 'like' does not appear in the answer. If you use a noun, you need to use the word 'like' in the answer.

Subject + 'taste' / 'smell' / 'feel' / 'look' / ['be'] + adjective

Subject + 'taste' / 'smell' / 'feel' / 'look' + 'like' + noun

What does it taste like?
It is spicy.
It tastes spicy.
It tastes like chicken.

What does it feel like?
It is soft.
It feels soft.
It feels like velvet.

When you answer the question 'What does _____ look like?', the answer does not usually include the word 'look' if you are using adjectives.

What does she look like?

She's tall and beautiful.

For the verbs 'taste', 'smell', 'feel' and 'look', we can also use 'How?' We answer the same way.

How does it taste?
It is spicy.
It tastes spicy.
It tastes like chicken.

COMPARISONS WITH MUCH, MANY, A LOT, A LITTLE, AND A BIT

'Much' or 'a lot' can be used to show that there is a big difference between two people or things.
'A little' or 'a bit' can be used to show a small difference.

With adjectives:

Austrians are much more formal than Swedes, and they are much less direct.

Austria is a bit cheaper than Sweden.

Remember that we cannot use a double comparative.

Right: Austrian food is much heavier.

Wrong: Austrian food is much more heavier.

With adverbs:

She speaks a little more quietly than I do.

He drives a lot faster than I do.

With nouns:

If the noun is uncountable, we use 'much' or 'a lot' (for a big difference), and 'a little' or 'a bit' (for a small difference).

In Sweden, they eat a lot more fish. They have much less daylight in winter.

If the noun is countable, we use 'many' or 'a lot' (for a big difference), and 'a few' for a small difference.

There are many more jobs in Sweden.

There are a few more taxis in New York than London.

Use 'fewer' to compare countable nouns and 'less' to compare uncountable nouns.

There are many fewer hours of daylight in a Swedish winter.

In Sweden, they have much less daylight in winter.

INTONATION IN QUESTIONS

When we ask questions, we can use different intonation patterns.

Sometimes we use a rising tone, sometimes we use a falling tone, and sometimes we use both.

When we ask questions beginning with a question word ('who', 'what', 'where', etc.), we use falling intonation.

Where are you from? What time is it?

When we ask a question without a question word, we use rising intonation.

Are you from Korea? Do you live in the city?

If we ask about a choice, we use a rising and falling pattern.

Do you prefer Italian food or Chinese food?

# of life

A Get into a group with three classmates. Think of 26 adjectives to describe people—one for each letter of the alphabet. How many can you think of in 60 seconds?

B Choose a partner and practise saying these tongue twisters to each other. Which is the most difficult to pronounce? Why?

- The sixth sick sheik's sixth sheep's sick.
- Three free throws
- Four fat frogs fly past five times.
- The two-twenty-two train tore through the tunnel.
- Say this sixteen times in succession.
- Sixish

- One-one was a racehorse,
  Two-two was one, too.
  When one-one won one race,
  Two-two won one, too.

C What sounds do you find difficult to pronounce in English? Think of some words that contain these sounds. Then write a tongue twister of your own.

Listening and Speaking

A This unit is about the different 'stages of life'. Discuss what you think that means with a partner and then share your ideas with the class.

B How many meanings do you know for the word 'stage'? Look at the following sentences, which use the word in different contexts. Can you match the alternative words to the correct sentence? Each sentence has three alternative words.

1 He's very shy. He'll never go to a karaoke bar and sing on stage. _____

2 Have you heard? The theatre is going to stage a new production of *Les Misérables*. _____

3 I'm never going to finish the project on time. At this stage, I'd rather give up and stop trying. _____

time	put on	present
phase	platform	do
stand	point	podium

C Here are some stages of life. Can you think of any others? Can you place them on the time line according to your own stage of life?

D Does our personality change with age? Which adjectives do you think best describe each age group? Choose adjectives for each picture. You can use each adjective as many times as you like. Use a dictionary to check the meaning of any new words.

a innocent, **b** mischievous, **c** inquisitive, **d** naughty, **e** selfish, **f** reckless, **g** practical, **h** confused, **i** bored, **j** doubtful, **k** settled, **l** stubborn, **m** retired, **n** adventurous, **o** confident, **p** content, **q** experienced, **r** irresponsible, **s** independent, **t** insecure, **u** mature, **v** naïve, **w** responsible, **x** self-assured, **y** timid, **z** wise

past   present   future

child, senior citizen, baby, middle-aged person, teenager, toddler, young adult

E Get into groups. Compare your answers with your classmates'. Discuss your choice of adjectives for each picture. Focus on the choices that were different.

F You are going to listen to Judy and Patrick talking about their attitudes towards getting older. Before you listen, match these idiomatic expressions from the conversation to their meaning.

1	The biological clock is ticking away.	☐	☐	a	I'm getting old.
2	I was sort of behind myself age-wise.	☐	☐	b	approximately aged 20–23
3	in my early 20s	☐	☐	c	For a woman, if you are worried about being too old to have children.
4	At the time, I thought I was wise.	☐			
5	I'm getting on a bit.	☐	☐	d	I acted younger than my real age.
			☐	e	In the past, I thought something, but now I know differently.

G Listen to Judy and Patrick. Look at the adjectives in Exercise D. Circle the ones you hear. Now listen again and put the adjectives you have circled under 'Younger' and 'Now' in the table below. Under 'Future' think of your own answers. Then answer the questions below.

	Younger	Now	Future
Judy			
Patrick			

1 Do Judy and Patrick feel positive or negative about getting older?
2 How old do you think Judy and Patrick are now?
3 How do your own ideas about getting older compare to Judy and Patrick's?

H Answer these questions, then discuss your ideas with the rest of the class.

1 What excites you the most about getting older?
2 What scares you the most?
3 What will you be able to do that you can't do now?
4 What won't you be able to do?
5 What do you think will never change about your personality, no matter how old you get?
6 What do you hope will change about your personality?

Grammar

A Thomas and Sergi are roommates and friends at EF Miami Beach. Read their conversation about plans for this weekend.

Sergi:	Hey, Thomas. Are you going to come with me to Disneyworld and Universal Studios this weekend? I'm going on the Orlando trip with the school.
Thomas:	That sounds like fun. Is it expensive?
Sergi:	Actually, it's very reasonable. It only cost me $200. The price includes transportation, accommodation, breakfast and tickets to the two parks.
Thomas:	Wow! That is a good deal. Oh, but wait. I can't. I already have plans.
Sergi:	What plans? What are you going to do this weekend?
Thomas:	I'm going to visit my cousins in Fort Lauderdale. I promised.
Sergi:	But this is my last weekend here before I go back home. This is our last chance to go together.
Thomas:	Well, maybe I can go to visit my cousins next weekend instead. I'll call them and explain the situation. I'm sure they'll understand.
Sergi:	Great. I can't wait. Don't forget to pay the activities coordinator before five o'clock. There aren't that many places left. Can you do it now?
Thomas:	No, I can't. I have a full schedule today. I'm going to be in classes until 4:00. I'll go to pay for the trip then.
Sergi:	OK. Well, I'm going to work out at the gym. I'm already late. But I'll see you when I get back.
Thomas:	OK. I'll see you later.

B Thomas and Sergi are talking about the future. Answer these questions about their plans.

1 Underline all the future forms in the text.
2 What two future forms are mostly used in the text? _____
3 Compare your answers to your partner's. Discuss why you think the two forms are being used.
4 Look at the text again. Write the future activities that were planned in the table below. Then write how you know it's a plan next to it.

plan	evidence
I'm going on the Orlando trip with the school.	It only cost me $200.

We usually use _____ when we talk about future _____.
We use _____ when we make a spontaneous _____ about the _____.

C On the chart below, write what you are planning to do next month. If you have no plans, imagine something fun!

plans

D Work with your partner. Ask each other questions about your future plans.

> **EXAMPLE**
> A: What are you going to do next month?
> B: I'm going to travel around Australia.

E Sometimes plans don't work out the way we want. So we have to make new plans. Tell your partner one of your plans. Your partner will tell you about a problem with your plan. Then you should make a new plan using 'will'.

> **EXAMPLE**
> A: I'm going to visit my friends in London next month.
> B: But that's the coldest month of the year!
> A: Oh! Then I think I'll visit my friends in Spain instead.

F Here are some other ways to talk about future plans. Which are usually used for plans that have already been made and which are usually used for plans that are not definite yet? I think I'll ... / I'd like to ... / I want to ... / I intend to ... / I'm definitely going to ... / I plan to ...

Definite plans	Indefinite plans

G Your parents, or other family members, are coming to visit you at EF for a week. Plan the week in the following diary. Don't forget to show them the really great things about your city. And don't forget your classes!

MON	TUE
WED	**THU**
FRI	**SAT**
SUN	

H Tell your partner about the week you have planned. Ask your partner to tell you about their plan. Remember to use the appropriate future forms for definite and indefinite plans.

> **EXAMPLES**
> We're definitely going to try out the 'London Eye'.
> Where are you going to take your family?

Writing and Grammar

A The time when people go to college or university is another important stage in life. This is the time when most of us learn to be independent and form and express our own ideas.

Julie is a very busy university student. Read her letter to her sister talking about her university life.

B Circle all the time conjunctions you can find in the letter, for example, 'while', 'as soon as'.

Underline the clauses the conjunctions join. Which sentences talk about the past? Which are about the present? Which are about the future? What tense is each clause in?

New York, April 14th

Dear Vicky

Hi! How are you? I'm sorry I haven't written in ages. I've been so busy with classes and work and everything. Life's pretty good here. I had a really good time last weekend, even though it didn't start very well! When I left work on Friday night, I was absolutely exhausted, and as soon as I got home, I fell asleep! I completely forgot that Naomi had asked me to baby-sit her son at 7:30. She called me at 7:30 to find out where I was. As soon as she called, I jumped out of bed and rushed over there. I made it in ten minutes and Naomi managed to get to her evening class in time. I felt so bad for causing her all that stress, but it worked out in the end.

Anyway, remember I told you about that really cute guy who works at the coffee shop? Well, on Saturday, we went out for lunch. Before I went out, I felt so nervous but we actually had a really good time. Our train was cancelled and we had to wait for an hour for the next train. While we were waiting, we talked a lot. He's a really nice guy and I'd like to see him again soon. But I'm really busy and I won't have time to see him until we have lunch together again next month.

Well, before my exams, I'm going to study really hard. I'm working while I'm studying to try to make ends meet. When I finish this term, I want to take a break! And after that, I think I'll run for class president. I know. I know. I have way too much ambition for a young woman my age.

Anyway, I hope you're well. Say 'hi' to Mum for me!

Love

Julie

C Put the following events on a time line to show the order of Julie's activities.

speak to Naomi	come home	go to sleep	finish course	meet guy	feel tired
go to Naomi's house	baby-sit	run for class president	take a break	wait for the train	
talk with the guy	finish work	study hard	take exams	have lunch	

Friday   Saturday   Future

D Complete the following sentences with your own ideas. Then compare your ideas with a partner's.

1 I _____ when I _____ .
2 When she _____ , she'll _____ .
3 While you're _____ , I'll _____ .
4 I _____ while I _____ .
5 As soon as I _____ , I _____ .
6 I'll _____ as soon as I _____ .
7 I didn't _____ until I _____ .
8 She won't _____ until she _____ .
9 After I _____ , I _____ .
10 Before _____ , I _____ .

E You are going to write a letter to a close friend or family member about your experiences at EF. Think about ten events to include in your letter. Include events from the recent past, the present and some things you plan to do in the near future. List the events in order. Think about how you will connect the events with conjunctions of time.

1 _____
2 _____
3 _____
4 _____
5 _____
6 _____
7 _____
8 _____
9 _____
10 _____

F Now, on a separate sheet of paper, write the letter. Use your list and Julie's letter in Exercise A as a guide.

G Get into groups of three. Read your letters to each other, one at a time. Listen to the other letters and fill in a time line for both. Then compare your answers. Did you all agree? Are any sentences too long or confusing? Work with your group to correct any mistakes and improve your letter.

H Choose one of your group's letters to read to the rest of the class. Write any suggestions on how to improve the letter below. Pay attention to comments on the future tenses and conjunctions of time.

past   present   future

Writing and Speaking

A No matter what stage of life you are at, there are products you will want to buy and companies who will want to sell their products to you. Do you remember the different stages of life? Write the name of each stage above the picture.

B Get into a group. In your group, brainstorm the type of products which are marketed at each age group. Write your ideas in the space below each picture.

C Now compare your ideas with the other groups'. Are there any products which are marketed at all age groups? Are there any products which are targeted only at people from one stage of life?

Baby Milk

fun

NEW

Your ticket to the best worldwide holiday destinations. The best places at the best times from day trips to extended trips.

family car

comfortable

D Now choose one of the types of products you have discussed. Then choose a specific product within the type of products. In your group, go on the Internet or look through magazines to search for advertisements for this product. Answer the following questions in your group.

1 Can you tell which age group advertisements for this product are targeted at? How?
2 Does this product appeal to people from more than one stage of life? If so, which ones?
3 Is the design of the advertisements appealing to a particular age group? Why?
4 What words and phrases are used to make this product look attractive?
5 How could the advertisements be changed to make the product appeal to people from different stages of life?
6 If the advertisements are targeted at your own age group, how successful do you think they are? How could they be improved?

E Still in your group, create a completely new advertisement for the product you have chosen. First, decide whether you are going to target it at one age group, or try to make it appeal to people from as many stages of life as possible. Think about the words and phrases you will use and then create your advertisement.

F Present your advertisement to the class. Explain your choice of language and design. Ask the class for feedback on your work.

G Advertisements can be a controversial subject. Here are some issues that it may be appropriate to talk about. Try to think of a few more to add to the list.

- Should cigarette advertisements be targeted at teenagers?
- Should adverts for products like alcohol and cigarettes be banned?
- Is it wrong to use images which may offend people (religious images or images of violence or nudity, for example) in advertising?
- Advertising is targeted mainly at young people and makes older people feel left out.
- Advertisements feature too many images of beautiful, thin people, encouraging 'ordinary' people to feel bad about themselves.
- Advertisements for beauty products are mostly lies.

Writing and Speaking

H In your group, discuss and note what your approach and position will be for debating each of the issues.

I When we debate, we use common expressions for agreeing and disagreeing. Look at the expressions below. Write a 'D' next to the expressions we use to disagree, 'A' next to those we use to agree and 'O' next to those we use for expressing an opinion.

     O   In my opinion ...

     A   I think so, too.

     D   That's out of the question!

_____ I believe ...

_____ I really feel that ...

_____ That's fine, but ...

_____ Yes, definitely.

_____ That's true, and ...

_____ It's my belief that ...

_____ Do you think so? I think ...

_____ That's ridiculous!

_____ That's fine, and ...

_____ That's true, but ...

_____ I don't think so.

_____ That's totally impossible!

_____ You're absolutely right.

_____ That's (exactly) what I think.

J Which are used to agree or disagree strongly? How can you make them more polite?

K Listen to your teacher read the expressions. Mark the stressed words in each expression. What happens to the meaning of the sentences when you stress these words very strongly? Practise with a partner.

L Now find a partner from another group and debate the issues. Try to convince your partner of your opinion. Use as many of the previous expressions as you can. Put a tick (✓) next to the ones that you use.

A You are going to read an article titled
Time flies when you're 41.
What do you think the article is going to be
about? Share your ideas with the class. Then
quickly scan the article to see if your ideas were
correct.

B Read the article.

Time flies when you're 41

We can't change the fact that we are all aging.
It's a fact of life that most of us hate dealing with.
It probably bothers us because we understand
that not everything is under our control. And once
we realise that, we must also confront our own
mortality.

As people reach their 40s and 50s, they start
to ask themselves what they've done so far and
what will lie ahead. It's more commonly known as
a 'mid-life crisis'. 'Am I having a mid-life crisis?'
is a question many people fret about when they
reach their middle years. This is the time when
we tend to reflect on what we haven't achieved,
where we haven't been, who we haven't met and,
in general, what we haven't done.

These days, even people in their 20s and 30s
have problems with the aging process. Many
people at this stage of life experience what is
known as 'a quarter-life crisis', when they worry
about whether they have chosen the right career,
if they are earning enough money, and whether or
not to get married and have children.

While some experts attribute these experiences to
physical changes in the body, others say it's more
emotional. Whether it's caused by realising there
are more years behind than there are ahead or
by hormone levels shifting, these are still difficult
stages in anyone's life. Although not everyone will
be affected, it's not uncommon for both women and
men to go through some kind of age-related crisis.

We all know the clichés about people impulsively
quitting their jobs, buying red sports cars and
trading in older spouses for younger and 'newer'
partners. We also know how some people can
fall into a period of depression. But that doesn't
necessarily need to be the case. Mid-life doesn't
have to be a crisis, and nor does approaching your
thirtieth birthday. These should be times to take
stock and reexamine your life, to revisit old dreams
and plan new ways to fulfil personal goals.

C Find the word or words in the text that mean the following:

a time passes quickly *time flies*
b to handle *to deal with*
c to face up to *confront*
d death at the end of life *mortality*
e to worry *to fret*
f to be most likely to do *tend*
g to think and wonder about *to reflect*
h to connect *to attribute*

i to change *shifting*
j an obvious statement or remark *clichés*
k to do something spontaneously *impulsively*
l to exchange *trading in*
m husband or wife *spouse/partner*
n a time, situation or circumstance *period*
o to evaluate *reexamine*
p to accomplish *fulfill*

Reading and Speaking

D Use the following table to see how you could handle some of the problems associated with aging. In the first column, write important areas of your life (career, marriage, etc). In the second column, write down troubling issues for each category. Then write plans for overcoming each issue in the third column. When you have finished, get into groups and discuss your ideas.

life	problems	plans

E Imagine you are having an age-related crisis. You are confused and need to talk. Here are some people you might talk to about your problems. How would you talk to each person about your concerns? What would be the same in the conversations? What would be different? Work with a partner and write down your ideas.

spouse _____

best friend _____

work colleague _____

child _____

parent _____

F Now choose one of the situations in Exercise E and create a dialogue with your partner. Don't forget to use the correct forms when you talk about your definite or indefinite plans, spontaneous decisions and guesses about the future.

G Practise the dialogue with your partner and then present it to the rest of the class.

H In a group, write ten questions to ask people about turning thirty or being middle-aged. Write your questions on the board. (Remember that people can be sensitive about their age. Make sure your questions are polite.)

I Look at the questions on the board and, as a class, decide which questions are the best and most important. Create a questionnaire and find two people outside of the classroom to interview. Make sure one person is younger and one is older. Report your findings to the class.

Homework

Write a report about people's reactions to turning thirty or being middle-aged, based on the information collected by the class.

Reading

A Look at the title of the article below.

Why I'm choosing to go grey

Read these questions and discuss your ideas with a partner.
What age do you think the author is?
Do you think the author is a man or woman? Why?
What do you think the main point of the article will be?
What possible reasons are there for wanting to go grey?

B Scan the article to see if your ideas were correct. Don't read the article in depth yet.

C This article has four paragraphs. Number them in the correct order.

But when it comes down to it, I know I'm going to stay grey. I'd rather have more grey than be a woman who's afraid of aging. I may look older but I still have my principles. The lipstick. The passion for life. The hair. It's a great look. _____

When I turned 30, I started pulling out white hairs. Now, at 35, there are too many to pull out and people have started to ask if the grey bothers me. I usually answer, 'Yes, but only a bit.' _____

I like grey hair on women. It looks attractive and really great if you're wearing lipstick. It's obviously natural. Women with long grey hair look smart and powerful. They look like they are in love with life. Women who choose not to dye their hair stand out as people of courage. _____

So why does having grey hair worry me? Well, it worries me because I am a bit afraid of looking older than I really am. It bothers me that something so unimportant can be such a hard decision. _____

D Read the article. Work with your partner. Discuss the following questions.

1 What does the author think is good about going grey?
2 In which paragraph(s) does she mention this?
3 Why does going grey worry her?
4 In which paragraph(s) does she talk about this?
5 What is the main idea of this article?
6 In which paragraph(s) does she mention this?
7 What other things might bother you about your appearance as you get older? Are there different issues for men and women?
8 Do you think the article is well organised or would you organise it differently?

E 'Stand out' is used in the article. What does it mean? Do you know any other phrasal verbs with 'stand'?

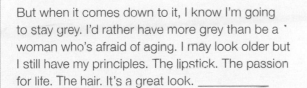

Language Practice

A Fill the gaps with the following phrasal verbs. Use the correct forms.

stand out	stand up	stand by	stand back	stand for

1 'e.g.' _____ 'for example' and 'USA' _____ 'The United States of America'.
2 (On the train platform) 'Please _____ because there is a train coming.'
3 We always _____ when we sing the National Anthem.
4 He always felt different from the other children. He _____ because he was the only child who couldn't hear.
5 (In a TV studio) 'OK. Everybody _____. We are going to go live in five seconds.'

B Phrasal verbs are a very important part of the English language. They are used very often. Look back over the unit, find as many phrasal verbs as you can and write them in the table below. Then compare your phrasal verbs with your partner's. Did you find the same ones?

phrasal verbs	'regular' verbs

C Work with your partner and try to find a 'regular' verb that has the same meaning. Write them next to the phrasal verbs in the table.

D Choose three of the phrasal verbs and create sentences with them. Read your sentences to the rest of the class, without the phrasal verb, and let them guess which one should be used.

E Throughout this unit, we have discussed the different stages of life. When we talk about our age, events in our life and plans, we often need to use different forms of numbers. Listen and mark the stress on these numbers.

- thirteen / thirteenth / thirty / thirtieth / thirties
- fourteen / fourteenth / forty / fortieth / forties
- fifteen / fifteenth / fifty / fiftieth / fifties
- sixteen / sixteenth / sixty / sixtieth / sixties
- seventeen / seventeenth / seventy / seventieth / seventies
- eighteen / eighteenth / eighty / eightieth / eighties
- nineteen / nineteenth / ninety / ninetieth / nineties

F What else do we have to be careful about when saying these numbers?

G Choose five numbers and write them below.

_____

Read your numbers to your partner, but don't show them to him / her. Write the numbers your partner says below.

_____

H Join the sentences.

1 Before I go home tonight, ☐
2 When I was at school, ☐
3 As soon as I have enough money, ☐
4 When I retire, ☐
5 I didn't like classical music ☐
6 After I finish work, ☐

☐ a I usually go to the pool.
☐ b I'm going to buy a computer.
☐ c until I was in my 20s.
☐ d I wanted to be a nurse.
☐ e I want to travel around the world.
☐ f I have to correct all these papers.

I Correct the mistakes in the following letter.

When I'll finish college, I'd like to go travelling. The problem is that I don't have enough money so while going travelling, I'll have to get a better-paid job. I really want to see Thailand, so I think I'm going to take a few Thai classes this summer after I'm going to finish my exams. I'd like to start sooner but I can't do anything as soon as I finish my exams. Before to do anything, though, I must complete my final paper for my philosophy class.

J Fill the gaps with the correct form of the verb in brackets.

1 When I _____ (retire), I want to _____ (live) somewhere by the sea.
2 I think _____ (go) shopping after I _____ (finish) work today.
3 I _____ (tell) you as soon as I _____ (hear) any news.
4 We _____ (not start) the meeting until you _____ (arrive).
5 When I _____ (be) at college, I _____ (be) very shy.
6 I _____ (not learn) to ride a bicycle until I _____ (be) 25.
7 I _____ (eat) dinner after I _____ (finish) my homework.
8 Please _____ (phone) me as soon as you _____ (hear) what's happened.
9 Do you think they _____ (visit) us before we _____ (go) on holiday?
10 When I _____ (get) older, I _____ (be) more confident.

K Put 'will' or 'going to' into each of the following dialogues with the correct form of the verb.

A: Why are you wearing your jacket?
B: Because I _____ (go) shopping with a friend.

A: I think we are lost!
B: Well, let's ask for directions. I _____ (find) a policeman.

A: There's a fire in the kitchen!
B: Oh, no! I _____ (call) the fire brigade!

A: How are you going to go to school this afternoon?
B: Jack _____ (give) me a lift.
A: But his car is broken.
B: Oh! Well, I _____ (catch) a bus then.

A: The phone is ringing!
B: I _____ (get) it.

A: Why have you been working so hard lately?
B: Because I _____ (buy) a car and I need to save a lot of money.

A: Why have you got so many hot dogs, hamburgers and steaks?
B: Because I _____ (have) a barbecue this weekend.

A: I don't have enough money to take the bus home.
B: I _____ (lend) you some, if you like. How much do you need?
A: Three pounds should be enough. I _____ (give) it back tomorrow.

Language Reference

TALKING ABOUT THE FUTURE WITH 'WILL' AND 'GOING TO'

We often use 'will' and 'going to' to talk about the future.

We usually use 'going to' when we talk about future plans.

We use 'will' when we make a spontaneous decision about the future.

A: *I'm going to visit my uncle in Toronto this weekend.* (plan)

B: *But there's an airline strike this week.*

A: *Really? Well, I guess I'll visit him some other time, then.* (new spontaneous decision)

We use 'will' to talk about what we think will happen in the future. If we want to talk about our own plans, we can also use 'I think I'll …', 'I'd like to…' or 'I want to…' when the plan isn't definite yet.

She'll fail the exam if she doesn't study harder.

I think I'll go out for a walk this evening.

I want to go and see a film tomorrow.

We can use 'I intend to…' or 'I plan to…' for plans that have already been made.

I plan to study politics when I go to Cambridge University.

They intend to fly to Beijing, and then take the train to Shanghai.

Note: 'will' can also be used to show determination and certainty if it is stressed in a sentence.

I will come and there's nothing you can do to stop me!

CONJUNCTIONS OF TIME

We can join two sentences using a conjunction.

A conjunction of time gives us information about when two events happen, relative to each other.

Common conjunctions are 'when', 'while', 'as soon as', 'until', 'after' and 'before'.

'When' can be used to show that one event is before, or at the same time as another. 'When' can be used in the past or the future.

I studied abroad for a year when I was at university.

When she finishes this course, she'll go abroad for a year.

'While' can be used to show that two things happen at the same time.

While you're getting lunch ready, I'll wash the car.

I studied judo while I was in Japan.

'As soon as' shows that the second event happened, or will happen, very soon after the first.

As soon as I finished lunch, I went out for a walk.

I'll go out for a walk as soon as I finish lunch.

In the second example, the verb 'finish' is in the simple present but has a future meaning.

'Not…until' means the same as 'not…before'.

I didn't leave home until I got married.

'After' and 'before' can be followed by a clause or by a gerund.

After I had eaten five ice-creams, I felt a little sick.

Before coming back to Britain, I travelled all over Eastern Europe.

a deal

After this unit, you should be able to ...

- Use 'make' and 'do' expressions
- Negotiate a good deal
- Identify collocations related to negotiating
- Recognise and use language to avoid cultural stereotyping
- Use topic sentences in writing

A People negotiate in many different situations. In which of these situations have you negotiated? Do people negotiate differently in different cultures?

1 a customer in a shop
2 someone buying a car
3 a team of peacekeepers talking to two countries at war
4 a student buying a language course
5 an employee requesting a week's vacation
6 a child and his parents talking about what time bedtime is
7 a doctor prescribing some medication to a patient
8 a lawyer discussing his client's court case with a judge

B Stand up and talk to your classmates. Try to persuade someone to ...

- lend you a pen
- have lunch with you
- buy you a coffee
- walk home from class with you

C How successful were you at persuading your classmates?
Note down the language that helped you to get what you wanted.

Listening and Speaking

A These words are often used to talk about negotiating. Match each word to the correct definition.

1	a strategy	▢	▢	a	to believe something is true without checking if it is really true
2	a goal	▢	▢	b	an idea; a possible answer
3	a suggestion	▢	▢	c	another choice
4	an alternative	▢	▢	d	a plan
5	a compromise	▢	▢	e	a target or aim
6	a reason	▢	▢	f	to give an explanation for your opinion; to show it makes sense
7	negotiation(s)	▢	▢	g	a discussion in which two sides try to reach an agreement
8	to justify an argument	▢	▢	h	a cause or an explanation
9	to assume something	▢	▢	i	an agreement made between two opposites, in the middle

B Which of the nouns 1-6 in Exercise A collocate with these verbs? Fill in the chart.
After you have finished, check your answers and then answer the questions below.

make	have	reach	give	offer

What nouns are made from the two verbs, 'to justify' and 'to assume'?
Which verbs in the chart do they collocate with?
What collocations do you know for 'negotiation' or 'negotiations'?

C In your opinion, what makes a good negotiator? Use the collocations that you
learnt to make a list. You can make positive and negative statements.

A good negotiator ...

D A consultant is going to give a presentation about what makes a good negotiator. Listen for the main points and number them in the correct order.

_____ What makes a good negotiator: repeating reasons and checking understanding?

_____ What makes a good negotiator: giving alternatives and making compromises?

_____ Questions this presentation will answer.

_____ What makes a good negotiator: having a long-term view?

What are the two types of negotiator the speaker contrasts to make his argument?

E Imagine you are negotiating with your boss for a pay rise. With a partner, discuss which strategy in each pair would be most successful and why.

1 _____ Keep quiet about your achievements.
  _____ Tell your boss what you have achieved since you joined the company.

2 _____ Say why you deserve a pay rise.
  _____ Complain about how much you are paid.

3 _____ Be aggressive and confident.
  _____ Be polite and gentle.

4 _____ Present your requirements as single points.
  _____ Present your requirements with alternatives.

5 _____ Be prepared to make compromises.
  _____ Don't make compromises.

6 _____ Repeat your reasons many times during the negotiation.
  _____ Give your reasons only once during the negotiation.

7 _____ Justify your arguments with lots of reasons.
  _____ Justify your arguments with only one or two reasons.

8 _____ Check often that your boss understands.
  _____ Assume that your boss understands.

F Look at the arguments in Exercise E and answer the questions.

1 Why is it important to offer alternatives when you present a goal?
2 Why is it necessary to make compromises?
3 How do these things make a negotiation successful?
4 Can you think of a time when you made a compromise to get something you wanted?

G A formal presentation is similar to a written essay. It has an introduction, usually two to three main points, and a conclusion. Imagine that you are going to make a formal presentation about what makes a good friend. Make some notes.

What makes a good friend	What doesn't make a good friend

H Now write an outline to organise your thoughts.

Introduction: This presentation is about ...
Part 1: The key factors that make a good friend

_____
_____
_____

Part 2: Things a good friend would never do

_____
_____
_____

Conclusion: To summarise ...

_____
_____
_____

I Write your complete presentation. Practise saying it out loud to yourself. Then find a partner and practise your presentation in front of him / her to gain confidence.

J Give your presentation to the rest of the class. Students who are listening should take notes to answer the question.

What are the key words that tell you what makes a good friend?

Pronunciation

 A There are many English words that end in '-sion' and '-tion'.

Some are pronounced with the /ʃ/ sound.

┏━■ EXAMPLE ━━━━━━━━━━━━━━━━━━━┓
accommodation
┗━━━━━━━━━━━━━━━━━━━━━━━━━━━┛

Others are pronounced with the /ʒ/ sound.

┏━■ EXAMPLE ━━━━━━━━━━━━━━━━━━━┓
revision
┗━━━━━━━━━━━━━━━━━━━━━━━━━━━┛

Listen to the words and circle the correct sound.

eg	*accommodation*	(ʃ)	3
eg	*revision*	ʃ	(3)
1	television	ʃ	3
2	ambition	ʃ	3
3	assumption	ʃ	3
4	cancellation	ʃ	3
5	collision	ʃ	3
6	condition	ʃ	3
7	conversation	ʃ	3
8	decision	ʃ	3
9	demonstration	ʃ	3
10	description	ʃ	3
11	explosion	ʃ	3
12	information	ʃ	3
13	invasion	ʃ	3
14	negotiation	ʃ	3
15	occasion	ʃ	3
16	presentation	ʃ	3
17	profession	ʃ	3
18	investigation	ʃ	3

 B Listen again and repeat each word.

C What is the difference between the two sounds? Is your mouth shape the same or different? Put your hand on your throat. Can you feel any difference?

D Write ten sentences using the words in Exercise A and practise saying these sentences. Check your partner's pronunciation.

1. _____
_____
2. _____
_____
3. _____
_____
4. _____
_____
5. _____
_____
6. _____
_____
7. _____
_____
8. _____
_____
9. _____
_____
10. _____
_____

 E Look again at the words in Exercise A. Underline all the stressed syllables. Listen again to check your answers.

F Here are three different stress patterns. Which words from Exercise A follow each pattern?

a • • **●** •
b **●** • • **●** •
c • **●** •

Reading and Writing

A Read the proverb and answer the questions.

'One man's meat is another man's poison.'

Thinking about negotiations between people of different cultures, what do you think the proverb could mean?
What examples of cultural differences that could cause problems between people can you think of?
Do you have personal experience with this, or do you know of any books or movies that have such examples?

B Read the cases of cross-cultural negotiation. What cultural differences do you think caused each problem? Choose the explanations on the next page. Write the correct letter(s) in the box.

Case 1 A Swede felt that a Spaniard was being aggressive and threatening during a negotiation about the cost of renting office space in Madrid. When he was asked why he felt this, he said it was because the Spaniard kept staring at him and making him feel uncomfortable. The Spaniard, on the other hand, felt that the Swede was not really interested in what he was proposing.

Case 2 Some Canadians negotiating with some Italians felt that the Italians were not interested in making a deal. The Italians arrived a quarter of an hour late, and the Canadians felt the meeting went on too long.

Case 3 A French company invited some Indonesians to France to discuss a contract. The French booked lunch and dinner at expensive restaurants during the two days of negotiation and were offended when the Indonesians did not want any lunch. The French also felt that the Indonesians lacked energy and enthusiasm. It was a stressful time for everyone. It was Ramadan in Indonesia at the time.

Case 4 A small team of Germans were negotiating with a North American businessman. Although the Germans spoke good English, both sides felt uncomfortable.

Case 5 A team of Australians negotiating in English in Japan thought they were doing really well. The Japanese in the meetings nodded a lot, said 'yes' often, and seemed to agree to all the proposals. In the end, however, they did not succeed in signing a contract.

Explanations about typical behaviour in different cultures

a It is acceptable to be a few minutes late for an appointment in Italy. In Italy, this is not usually interpreted as a lack of interest or commitment.

b British and North American people often cannot speak the language of the country they are visiting. On the other hand, many people whose first language is not English can speak at least a little English. Sometimes there is resentment at having to use the other person's language.

c The length of time for eye contact can be three times longer in Spain than in Sweden.

d Many Japanese people would feel it is very rude to ask others to repeat themselves. Even if they do not understand something, Japanese people may nod their heads.

e Muslim cultures observe a religious festival called Ramadan. During this time, they do not eat or drink while the sun is up. Not eating or drinking for such a long period of time can make a person seem tired.

f When a Japanese person says, 'Yes', it often means 'I understand', not 'I agree'. So a Japanese person nodding may not be showing that they agree, but only saying that they have heard and understood what the other person has said.

g In general, for North Americans, being on time is important. Being late for an important meeting is considered rude.

C Look at the pairs of sentences. Underline the words and expressions in the second sentences that make them sound less like stereotypes.

1 **a** British and North American people cannot speak another language.
  b British and North American people often cannot speak another language.

2 **a** Japanese people feel it is very rude to ask others to repeat themselves.
  b Many Japanese people would feel it is very rude to ask others to repeat themselves.

3 **a** Even if they do not understand, Japanese people nod their heads.
  b Even if they do not understand, Japanese people may nod their heads.

4 **a** In the Middle East, it is important to get to know people and establish a good relationship before negotiating or doing business.
  b In some countries in the Middle East, it is important to get to know people and establish a good relationship before negotiating or doing business.

5 **a** There is resentment at having to use the other person's language.
  b Sometimes there is resentment at having to use the other person's language.

6 **a** For North Americans, being on time is important.
  b In general, for North Americans, being on time is important.

Reading and Writing

D Rewrite these stereotypes to make them more culturally sensitive.

1 The French like to eat in expensive restaurants.
_____

2 Americans are only interested in short-term profit.
_____

3 Brazilians love football.
_____

4 Canadians prefer outdoor activities.
_____

5 Koreans think strict discipline is important.
_____

6 The British don't show their emotions.
_____

7 Australians travel all over the world.
_____

8 Swedes like to drink alcohol.
_____

9 The Japanese are very formal in business situations.
_____

E Write a list of behaviours that are common in the culture you are in now. Avoid stereotypes by using the expressions you have learnt in this lesson.

F Now write a letter to someone from another culture, telling them about the culture you are in now. Use some of the sentences you wrote in Exercise E. Ask some questions about cultural differences in your letter.

> ■ EXAMPLE
> *Dear Kari*
> *Here in the UK, British people are, in general, very friendly and polite.*
> *What are the people in Norway like?*

G Look again at Exercise B. What would you say to the people in each situation to help them do business more successfully?

1 The Swede and the Spaniard:
_____

2 The Canadians and the Italians:
_____

3 The French and the Indonesians:
_____

4 The Germans and the North American:
_____

5 The Australians and the Japanese:
_____

Speaking and Listening

A Do we use 'make' or 'do' with these words? Write 'm' or 'd'.

make / do			
a presentation	☐	research	☐
a compromise	☐	a suggestion	☐
a list	☐	a report	☐
your homework	☐	an assumption	☐
the laundry	☐	a deal	☐
the dishes	☐	sure	☐
the ironing	☐	a profit	☐
the vacuuming	☐	a decision	☐
conversation	☐	an offer	☐
a cake	☐	business	☐
a favour	☐	an effort	☐
an agreement	☐	a call	☐
a job	☐	your best	☐
everything again	☐	a mistake	☐
your bed	☐	the shopping	☐
revisions	☐	the cooking	☐

B In pairs, write a dialogue using as many 'make' and 'do' expressions as possible. Make sure your dialogue sounds natural.

C Listen to the conversation and answer the questions.

1 Who is speaking?

2 What does each person want?

3 What do they agree on?

4 Do you think the client got a good deal? Why or why not?

D Listen to the conversation again, and complete the sentences. Then answer the questions.

1 I'm _____ that _____ be possible. We don't have a double for five nights.

2 If you _____ three nights, we _____ give you a 5% discount.

3 _____ we stayed for four nights? _____ you have anything available?

4 No, I'm sorry. We wouldn't _____ do that for that price.

5 OK, _____ I _____ $275 a night. Would you include breakfast then?

6 We _____ give you a continental breakfast, but only if you _____ for it separately.

What expression do people often use to show they have reached an agreement? 'It's a _____.' What expressions can we use to make a proposal or negotiate? What verb forms can be used?

E Your teacher will divide you into groups and give each of you a card to play the Negotiation Game. You must negotiate with the other students in your group by using the information that is on your card. You must try and find other students who can make a deal with you.

> ■ EXAMPLES
>
> *Your card says: a cake / the dishes*
> *Student A says to Student B: 'If you made a cake, I would do the dishes.' OR*
> *'Supposing I did the dishes, would you make a cake?'*
>
> *If Student B has an exact match, they will say: 'It's a deal.'*
> *If Student B does not, they will say: 'I'm sorry, that won't be possible.'*

Speaking and Listening

F Negotiation is more successful if people use polite language. Compare the following sentences. Which is better for negotiating? Why?

- ☐ We want 400 cases of soda, and we want a cheap price.
- ☐ We would like to order 400 cases of soda. What kind of discount could you offer?

G Use what you have learnt about negotiating language to rewrite the dialogues.

1 A: We want to buy 5,000. Give us a discount.
   B: We will give you 5%. But you have to buy 6,000 like last time.
   A: We'll buy 8,000 for 10%.
   B: OK.

2 A: You must pay for the goods in thirty days.
   B: We can't. We want sixty days to pay.
   A: No way!
   B: Then we can't agree. Too bad!

H Role play using your negotiating skills.

Student A

1 You are a student at a language school. You missed the most recent test because you overslept because the time changed over the weekend. You don't want to get a zero. You want to have another chance to get a grade. Speak with your teacher and try to get him or her to give you another opportunity.

2 You are the best football player in your country. It is time to negotiate your contract again. You currently make $14,000,000 a year, but you want to make $20,000,000 a year because since you arrived on the team, every game has sold out.

3 You are 17 years old and have just passed your driving test. You also just graduated from high school with top grades. You want your parents to get you a car for your graduation.

Student B

1 You are a teacher. You have a strict policy about tests—if a student is absent, he or she fails. One student overslept because the time changed over the weekend, and now wants to make up the test. The student is normally a good worker, and you understand the situation; however, you don't want to create a new test.

2 You own a football team, and your best player needs to negotiate his contract again. He currently makes $14,000,000 a year, but he wants to make $20,000,000 a year. If you give him this salary, you will have to lose your goalkeeper, who has played very well this year.

3 You are a parent. Your 17-year-old child has just got his / her licence and graduated from high school with top grades. As a graduation gift, your child wants a car. You are concerned because a new car would be expensive, and you have two younger children. Also, you think that 17 is still too young to drive, especially with friends.

Reading and Speaking

A Skim read the article about China and answer the questions.

- What kind of changes have taken place since the 1980s?
- What still needs to be done?
- What challenges are there for western businesses?

1 _____ Since the 1980s, this market has been opening up more and more, and many western companies are setting up joint ventures with newly created private Chinese companies so that they can do business there.

2 _____ Contracts were made with overseas corporations to build western-style hotels for the increasing number of tourists and business executives from abroad.

3 _____ Thousands of kilometres of new roads and railways are needed, as are power stations to supply energy, and a communications system that can connect phones to millions more households. These huge projects offer exciting opportunities for foreign companies.

4 _____ While there are many opportunities, the Chinese way of doing business is different from that in the west, and companies should remember that it may take a long time, perhaps five years or more, to get results. This means that if you want to succeed in China, you need to have long-term commitment—and patience.

B Read the sentences and match them to the correct paragraph in Exercise A.

a Organisations hoping to succeed in this market should spend some time studying Chinese corporate and national culture.

b In the early 1980s, China recognised the benefits of a market economy and began importing goods from other countries.

c There are 1.3 billion people in China, making it one of the biggest potential markets in the world.

d Since the start of the 1990s, China's main priority has been to modernise industry and to prepare its infrastructure for the 21st century.

C Write three possible titles for the article.

D Circle the correct options. There may be more than one correct answer.

1 Western companies want to invest in China because ...
a China has many people who might buy western products in the future
b China's industry is modern
c western companies can make money by building hotels and infrastructure in China

2 China is helping western companies by ...
a creating new Chinese companies to work together with western companies
b opening up the economy so western goods can come into China
c improving its roads

3 Before the 1980s, western companies didn't invest in China because ...
a the telephones and roads weren't good
b the economy was closed
c you have to be patient to do business in China

4 The main idea of this entire text is ...
a China has a big potential market with opportunities for the right businesses
b Chinese business culture is still very different from western business culture
c China's infrastructure is improving

E Find the words in the article that match these definitions.

1 a possible place to sell something _____
2 a business set up between two companies _____
3 an economic system in which the price of goods is decided by supply and demand _____
4 to bring a product into a country _____
5 a formal agreement between two or more organisations _____
6 a large company _____
7 a high-level manager _____
8 the most important thing _____
9 transport systems, communications systems, power and water supplies, etc _____
10 a willingness to have a relationship for a long time _____

F Discuss these questions.

1 What does the article say about China's economy since the 1980s?
2 Why would western companies invest in China?
3 Why is China opening its economy to western investors?

G The first sentence in each of the paragraphs in the article on China on page 43 is the topic sentence. Look back at the China article and answer the questions. What is the main idea of each paragraph?

H A topic sentence is made up of two parts—the topic and the controlling idea. Read the paragraph below and the example. What does a topic sentence do?

A successful negotiator has three important characteristics. First, while engaging in negotiations, he or she offers alternatives, not demands. That way, the other side has options to work with. Second, a successful negotiator justifies his or her arguments with a few important reasons. It can be confusing to use too many reasons; a few good ones make an argument stronger. Finally, a successful negotiator is always prepared to make compromises. Compromises are often necessary to reach an agreement.

> **■ EXAMPLE**
>
> *topic sentence: A successful negotiator has three important characteristics.*
> *topic: negotiation*
> *controlling idea: There are three characteristics of a successful negotiator.*

I You can use different controlling ideas with the same topic to create different topic sentences. Look at the three sentences below. They share the same topic, but their controlling ideas are different. (Notice that the topic can be in different places in the sentence.) Answer the questions.

◻ Negotiating is a skill that anyone can learn.
◻ When working with different cultures, negotiating can be challenging.
◻ Negotiating is an important part of making a deal.

1 What is the topic?
2 What are the controlling ideas?
3 What would you expect to read about if you saw these topic sentences?

J For each topic on the right, make three topic sentences with different controlling ideas. Remember that a topic sentence carries the main idea for a paragraph, so you need to be able to support your idea with more sentences.

> **■ EXAMPLE**
>
> *Our school is located at 123 Main Street.*
> *is NOT a topic sentence because it is simply a*
> *fact. There is nothing to support it.*

1 Our school

_____

_____

_____

2 Stereotypes

_____

_____

_____

3 Television

_____

_____

_____

K Choose one of the topic sentences you wrote in Exercise J and write a paragraph to support your topic sentence.

Language Practice

A Many words have a noun, a verb and an adjective form. It's helpful to learn all of the forms at the same time. It will help you increase your vocabulary. Complete the table below.

Noun	Verb	Adjective
accommodation	accommodate	accommodating
	X	ambitious
	assume	X
cancellation		X
collision		X
	converse	conversational
	decide	decisive
demonstration		demonstrative
description		
explosion	explode	
information	inform	
	invade	invasive
negotiation		X
presentation		X
	revise	X
	suggest	X
	televise	X

B Mark the stressed syllables in each word in Exercise A. Practise saying the words. Pay attention to the pronunciation of / ʃ / and / ʒ /.

C Rewrite these sentences, correcting the mistakes in them.

1 The cooking demonstrate went well until the pie exploded.

_____

2 Television can be very information.

_____

3 She descriptive the army's invade in great detail.

_____

4 He is very ambition. He has decision to become a doctor.

_____

5 When the two cars collision, there was a large crash, and then an explode.

_____

D Fill in the gaps with the correct forms of 'make' or 'do'.

1 I _____ an appointment yesterday to see the marketing manager.
2 Have you ever _____ a really difficult decision?
3 Our supplier _____ us a big favour last time. They delivered the machines free of charge.
4 We can offer a 10% discount, but we can't _____ much better than that, I'm afraid.
5 I couldn't _____ that phone call to our suppliers because the phone system was out of order.
6 Did you _____ some sightseeing on your last trip to Rome?
7 He always _____ ridiculous suggestions.
8 I forgot to _____ arrangements for a car to meet me at the airport. I had to take a taxi.

E Match each idiom with its definition.

1 make somebody's hair stand on end ☐   ☐ a to help someone
2 make yourself at home ☐   ☐ b to frighten somebody
3 do one's best ☐   ☐ c to go to prison or jail
4 do someone a favour ☐   ☐ d to research something carefully
5 do your own thing ☐   ☐ e to take a small problem and make it really big
6 make time ☐   ☐ f to be positive in a bad situation
7 do time ☐   ☐ g to find time to do something even if you are very busy
8 do your homework ☐   ☐ h to try as hard as you can
9 make a mountain out of a molehill ☐   ☐ i to feel comfortable in someone's house
10 make the best of something ☐   ☐ j to be independent

F Write a paragraph for foreign business people who want to do business in your country. What cultural conventions should they be aware of? How should they behave in formal and informal situations?

NEGOTIATING

We can use different expressions to negotiate. Most commonly, we use conditional structures to do this.

In very concrete situations, we often use the first conditional to make a proposal.

If you make my bed, I will sweep the floor.

Another common way to negotiate is by hypothesising. We can make proposals and suggest solutions in this way.

We can ask for a proposal using questions.

What did you have in mind?

What would you say to…?

What if we…?

We generally make hypothetical proposals using the second conditional:

'if' + simple past, 'would' / 'could' + base form of the verb

If we ordered six thousand, would you give us a discount?

If we paid cash, could you deliver the order today?

We can also use the same construction with 'Supposing…'

Supposing we ordered six thousand, would you give us a discount?

'MAKE' AND 'DO'

The verbs 'make' and 'do' are used in many expressions in English and can often be confused. There are no hard and fast rules for when to use these verbs, but there are some patterns that you can follow.

We often use 'make' with the meaning of 'construct' or 'create'.

to make a plan, a cake, etc

We often use 'do' to perform an action or task.

to do your homework, to do the laundry, to do something over again

There are many idiomatic expressions that don't follow the rules.

to do one's best, to make progress, to do one's job, to make a fortune, etc

you!

After this unit, you should be able to ...

- Discuss health and healthcare
- Compare alternative and traditional medicines
- Give advice
- Use prepositions after adjectives and verbs
- Write a paragraph with a topic sentence and examples
- Find stress on word syllables
- Use gerunds in sentences

A Complete the following sentences about healthcare in your country. Then discuss your answers with others. Find two similarities and two differences in your answers.

1 If I have a bad cold, I go to...
  a a doctor's surgery office
  b a hospital
  c somewhere else

2 If I break my leg, I go to ...
  a a doctor's surgery office
  b a hospital
  c somewhere else

3 My doctor...
  a gives me choices
  b always explains everything to me
  c tells me what to do without any choices

4 Healthcare costs are paid by...
  a private health insurance
  b government health insurance
  c the patient—I pay everything
  d the government—it's free

5 Medicine or drugs ...
  a are obtained with a prescription from a doctor
  b are obtained without a prescription from a doctor
  c are very expensive
  d are very cheap
  e are one fixed price

6 In my country...
  a many people use alternative medicine such as acupuncture, Chinese herbal medicine or aromatherapy
  b most people use conventional medicine
  c some people use alternative medicine
  d some people use alternative medicine if conventional medicine doesn't work

7 If I need an ambulance, the number I call is _____.

Speaking and Vocabulary

A Which of the following do you associate with conventional medicine and which with alternative medicine? Write 'C' for conventional and 'A' for alternative. Discuss your answers with your partner.

1 _____ massage   6 _____ needles
2 _____ aromatherapy   7 _____ injections
3 _____ surgery   8 _____ drugs / medicine
4 _____ an X-ray   9 _____ homeopathy
5 _____ herbs   10 _____ acupuncture

B Look at the following phrases. Next to each, write 'S' if it is a symptom and 'T' if it is a treatment.

1 _____ be itchy   9 _____ a stomachache   17 _____ put on weight   25 _____ go on a diet
2 _____ a cold   10 _____ lose weight   18 _____ an X-ray   26 _____ exercise
3 _____ a headache   11 _____ plastic surgery 19 _____ sneeze   27 _____ an operation
4 _____ a fever   12 _____ a bruise   20 _____ antibiotics   28 _____ painkillers
5 _____ a rash   13 _____ be hospitalised 21 _____ sprain   29 _____ stitches
6 _____ a sore throat 14 _____ a cough   22 _____ a bandage   30 _____ physiotherapy
7 _____ a backache   15 _____ acupuncture   23 _____ cough syrup   31 _____ pills
8 _____ insomnia   16 _____ a shot / an injection 24 _____ cream   32 _____ vitamins

C Put the nouns in Exercises A and B in the table below to make collocations with the verbs in the pink boxes.

get / have	prescribe	take	apply / put on

D What are some differences between alternative medicine and conventional medicine? What are some examples of the beliefs and techniques used for each? Discuss your ideas with your partner and complete the chart below comparing them.

Alternative medicine	Conventional medicine
treats the body as a whole	uses drugs

E Here are some commonly used phrases for advice. Label those used for asking for advice 'A', those for giving advice 'G' and those for receiving advice 'R'. Can you add any more phrases?

1 _____ What would you recommend?
2 _____ Have you thought about verb + '-ing' ...?
3 _____ I'll give it a try.
4 _____ You could try ...
5 _____ I think I'm ready to try ...
6 _____ You might try ...

_____
_____
_____

F Match each illness to its symptoms. Then choose a treatment.

Illness	S	T
1 a cold	☐	☐
2 a stomachache	☐	☐
3 a fever	☐	☐
4 a broken leg	☐	☐

Symptoms
a bruises, pain in the leg
b nausea, lose weight
c a cough, a sore throat
d high temperature, a headache

Treatment
a cough syrup
b drink water, rest
c antibiotics, rest
d an x-ray, painkillers

G Fill the gaps using the phrases from Exercise E.

1 A: _____
B: No, I hadn't thought about that.
Is acupuncture good?

2 A: _____
B: I would recommend a day's rest in bed. Then you should feel better tomorrow.

3 A: Why don't you drink some warm milk before going to bed?
B: _____

4 A: _____ stretching every hour to maintain good circulation.
B: All right. That's a good idea.

5 A: _____
alternative medicine.
B: Great. I think aromatherapy will be helpful for you.

H As a class, conduct a role play.

Student A
You are a doctor. You are going to treat some patients and need to give them the best advice possible to help them get better. Look at the list of symptoms and treatments in Exercise B to help you. The patients will be judging who is the best doctor, so be sure to listen carefully and think about what is best. Will you recommend an alternative treatment or a conventional one? Remember to use the language for asking for, giving and receiving advice that you have learnt.

Student B
Your teacher will assign you a health problem. Refer to the symptoms in Exercise B in order to describe your condition in detail. You must consult different doctors and judge who has the best recommendation for treating your illness. Remember to use the language for asking for, giving and receiving advice that you have learnt.

Listening and Grammar

A Match each type of alternative medicine to the correct description.

1 acupuncture ☐
2 aromatherapy ☐
3 heat therapy ☐
4 herbal medicine ☐
5 homeopathy ☐
6 light therapy ☐
7 massage ☐
8 meditation ☐
9 music therapy ☐
10 visualisation ☐

☐ a You focus on a word or on your breathing. You try not to think of anything else.
☐ b You sit in a hot bath or sauna.
☐ c Doctors put needles into your skin at different points on your body.
☐ d You take a very small amount of a drug that produces the same symptoms as your illness.
☐ e You imagine a situation, a place, or an object.
☐ f You drink tea or take pills or powders made from plants.
☐ g You breathe in oils made from plants.
☐ h Practitioners touch and rub your body.
☐ i You listen to music.
☐ j You sit in bright light.

B Do you know what the following health problems are? Use a dictionary to find out the meaning of those words you are unsure of. Are these health problems mental health problems or physical health problems? Put them in the correct column.

| allergies depression headaches muscle pain |
| arthritis ear infections high blood pressure |
| sinus infections colds fever insomnia stress |

| Mental | Physical |

C Work with a partner and tell him / her about any doctors or nurses you have met. Were they good at their job? In general, what makes a good doctor or nurse?

D Listen to the first conversation. In your opinion, is Paul a good doctor? Why or why not?

_____

_____

_____

E Now listen to all four conversations. Which type of alternative medicine is each person talking about? What do they say their form of medicine is helpful for? Use the vocabulary from Exercises A and B to complete the chart as you listen.

	Type of therapy	Helpful for treating
Paul		
John		
Harold		
Helen		

F Listen again for the adjectives below. What words come after them?

1 nervous _____
2 good _____
3 opposed _____
4 satisfied _____
5 interested _____

G What type of word comes after the adjectives?

H Fill the gaps with information about yourself. Discuss your answers with your partner. Try to find something you have in common.

1 I'd say I'm good at _____.
2 _____ isn't good for me.
3 Right now I'm a little worried about

_____.
4 I'm afraid of _____ and

_____.
5 I'm pleased with _____.
6 I sometimes get angry about _____.
7 I'm not satisfied with _____.
8 I sometimes get bored with _____.
9 I'm very interested in _____.
10 I get nervous about _____.

I You are moving into the dormitory at college. You have to write a short introduction about yourself for the Housing Office so that the staff members can find a roommate for you. Give them as much detail as possible so they can find a good match. Be sure to use verb and adjective combinations with prepositions. See the Language Reference on page 64 for more information.

> **EXAMPLES**
>
> *I am a very organised person, so I am good at organising parties or events.*
> *I'm very interested in football.*

J In groups, read each other's introductions. Try and find the best roommates for everyone.

Reading and Speaking

A   Read the following statements. Do you think they are True or False?

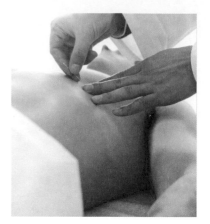

1   **T** **F**   Acupuncture became popular in China in the 1960s.
2   **T** **F**   Acupuncture is the only approach used in Chinese medicine.
3   **T** **F**   The idea of balance is important in conventional western medicine.
4   **T** **F**   'Yin' and 'yang' are two different kinds of energy.
5   **T** **F**   Chinese doctors often practise surgery to restore balance.
6   **T** **F**   Taking a patient's pulse is an important part of Chinese medicine.
7   **T** **F**   Western doctors use more laboratory tests than Chinese doctors.
8   **T** **F**   Most western doctors now practise Chinese medicine.

B   Read the article about acupuncture and check your answers.
How many questions did you get correct?

In Britain and North America, acupuncture is considered 'alternative medicine', a trendy approach to healing. In China, however, acupuncture is far from alternative. In fact, for the Chinese, nothing could be more traditional than acupuncture.

Acupuncture is one of many approaches used in Chinese medicine, and it is part of a 2,000-year-old tradition that differs greatly from conventional western medicine. According to western medicine, we are constantly being attacked by germs. Chinese medicine, on the other hand, focuses on the balance of two kinds of energy called 'yin' and 'yang'. When the energies of 'yin' and 'yang' are in balance, we are healthy. When the energies are out of balance, we become ill. A Chinese medical practitioner's job is to restore the balance of the energies. This is done with a combination of diet, acupuncture and herbal medicine.

Doctors of Chinese medicine are usually highly in tune with all aspects of their patients' well-being. When a patient goes to a doctor of Chinese medicine, the doctor often spends about 20 minutes taking the patient's pulse. The doctor also looks methodically at the patient's tongue and listens carefully to his / her breathing. They perform few of the laboratory tests which are common in western medicine.

Many western doctors have been sceptical about acupuncture and other Chinese approaches for a long time. It is difficult for western doctors to accept the idea of 'yin' and 'yang'; it is too different from the scientific traditions of western medicine. However, many people in the West are not worried about why Chinese medicine works. Chinese medicine has successfully treated a variety of health problems, including back pain, headaches, arthritis, and addiction. When people feel better, they do not always need to know the reason for their good health.

C   Match the words to their definitions. Use the text to check your answers.

1   approaches   ☐   ☐   a   fashionable
2   trendy   ☐   ☐   b   ways of doing things
3   tradition   ☐   ☐   c   old custom or opinion
4   germs   ☐   ☐   d   not believing in something easily
5   enemies   ☐   ☐   e   pays special attention to something
6   focuses   ☐   ☐   f   the beat caused by your heart pumping
7   pulse   ☐   ☐   g   people who want to hurt you
8   sceptical   ☐   ☐   h   very small organisms that cause illness

D What is the main idea put forward in the text about acupuncture? Write it in one complete sentence.

_____

_____

_____

E In an article or an essay, the thesis statement, or main controlling idea, is usually in the first paragraph. What is the thesis statement in this essay?

F In addition to a thesis statement, each paragraph has a topic sentence which states the main idea of the paragraph. Look for the topic sentences in Paragraphs 2, 3 and 4. What details are used to support them?

G Look at the article about acupuncture again. Try to find seven adjective + preposition or verb + preposition combinations. Some of the combinations have three words. What part of speech is the middle word?

1 _____ from

2 _____ on

3 _____ at

4 _____ to

5 _____ about

6 _____ from

7 _____ about

H Complete the following letter by choosing the correct preposition to follow the adjective or verb. Look at the Language Reference on page 64 for help.

Dear Jessica,

I'm concerned (1) _____ you. I was talking to Mum the other day, and she seemed worried (2) _____ the amount of time that you spend at work. I'd advise you (3) _____ becoming a workaholic. Dreaming (4) _____ being the best is fine, but getting addicted (5) _____ work is dangerous. Your health will suffer, and you won't have a social life. If your boss asks you to stay late more than a couple of times a week, insist (6) _____ having a little time to yourself. It's extremely important. I know it's hard to object (7) _____ what your boss says, but I believe deeply (8) _____ your ability to do what's right.

By the way, are you interested (9) _____ coming to visit me sometime soon? I'm not planning (10) _____ doing much, so just come and relax. You can always count (11) _____ me, you know. I look forward (12) _____ hearing from you soon.

Love,
Robin

Reading and Speaking

I Look at the letter in Exercise H on page 55 again. Underline all the '-ing' forms of the verbs. Some of these '-ing' forms are gerunds. You will learn more about these later in the unit.

J Decide with a partner, based on the reading and on your knowledge, whether the following statements refer to alternative or conventional medicine. If 'It' refers to alternative medicine, write 'A'. If 'It' refers to conventional medicine, write 'C'.

1 _____ It uses diet, exercise, and herbal medicines to treat illness.
2 _____ It focuses on the patient's personal experience of the illness.
3 _____ It treats the body like a machine that can have broken parts.
4 _____ It emphasises prevention of illness.
5 _____ It asks patients to obey and follow the doctor's orders.
6 _____ It tries to create balance in the mind and body.
7 _____ It relies on drugs and surgery to treat illness.
8 _____ It emphasises the treatment of specific illnesses.
9 _____ It fights against illness, almost like a war.
10 _____ It sees the body and mind as two separate things.

K Discuss the following questions in your group.

1 Have you ever tried acupuncture or other kinds of Chinese medicine? If so, were you satisfied with the results? If you haven't tried acupuncture, would you like to? Why or why not?

2 Would you go to a practitioner of Chinese medicine for ...?

- a cold
- a broken leg
- insomnia
- allergies

- back pain
- cancer
- heart disease
- pregnancy

3 Why do you think Chinese medicine and other kinds of alternative medicine have become so popular in western countries in recent years?

4 Do you know of any other ways of treating health problems? What kinds of medicine are used in your culture?

Homework

Review what you have learnt about the structure of essays in Exercises E and F. Using the article about acupuncture as a model, write a paragraph in which you compare the characteristics of alternative and conventional medicine. Remember to include details to support your main ideas.

Grammar, Vocabulary and Pronunciation

A How much do you know about living a healthy life? Take this quiz and find out. Read each statement and decide if it is True or False.

1 **T F** Sleeping more than seven hours a night helps people live longer.
2 **T F** Lifting weights is good for people over 70 years old.
3 **T F** Sleeping less than usual is a good idea when you have a lot of work to do.
4 **T F** Exercising at least once a week can improve your health.
5 **T F** 'Going cold turkey' (doing it all at once) is the best way to quit a bad habit.
6 **T F** Eating nuts increases your risk of heart disease.
7 **T F** Listening to music makes people work less efficiently.
8 **T F** Listening to loud music is helpful when you're exercising.
9 **T F** Being under stress increases the risk of catching a cold.
10 **T F** Getting better from a cold is out of your control.

B What do you notice about the subject of these sentences? What part of speech is it? When do we use it?

C Do you know the body parts in the box below? Work in pairs and point to each of these body parts on the diagram. Then label the diagram.

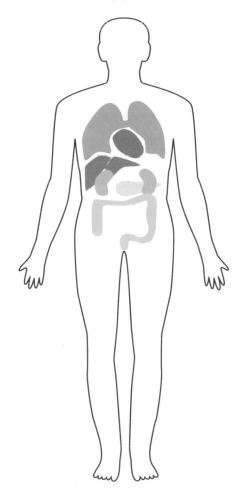

□ heart
□ lung
□ throat
□ stomach
□ liver
□ brain
□ tongue
□ spine
□ ankle
□ calf
□ thigh
□ elbow
□ wrist
□ kidney
□ thumb
□ shoulder

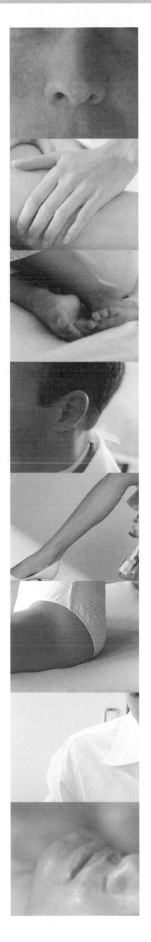

Grammar, Vocabulary and Pronunciation

D What is good for our bodies? What is bad for us? Write down at least six ideas. Practise using the gerunds from Exercise A on page 57.

> ■ EXAMPLE
> *Eating ginger is good for your digestion.*

1 _____   4 _____

2 _____   5 _____

3 _____   6 _____

E Complete the sentences with the correct form of the appropriate verb.

| increase   have   smoke   eat   combine   drink   bite |

1 _____ exercise with a healthy diet is the best way to lose weight.

2 Lung cancer is often caused by _____.

3 _____ too many sugary beverages may make you gain weight.

4 _____ fibre in your diet and _____ more whole grains can reduce the risk of developing diabetes.

5 _____ a community may be an important factor in living a healthy life.

6 One of my bad habits is _____ my nails.

F The sentences in Exercise E all contain gerunds. We can use a gerund as a subject, as an object, or as a complement in a sentence. Can you work out which sentences above fall into each category? Write the number of the sentence in the correct category.

Gerunds as subjects: _____

Gerunds as objects: _____

Gerunds as complements: _____

G Which of the following adjectives can be used to describe a cough, a fever, or pain? Complete the diagram with the adjectives below.

| chesty   high   slight   throbbing   sharp |
| dry   mild   severe   dull   terrible |

Cough   Pain

Fever

H When was the last time you had a cold or the flu? What were your symptoms? Tick which symptoms you had.

1 I had a runny nose. ☐
2 I had a cough. ☐
3 I had a fever. ☐
4 I had a sore throat. ☐
5 I lost my voice. ☐
6 I had an upset stomach. ☐
7 I threw up / vomited. ☐
8 I had diarrhoea. ☐
9 I sneezed a lot. ☐
10 I had aching joints. ☐
11 I had a migraine / headache. ☐
12 I had insomnia. ☐

I Listen and practise saying the words. One syllable is stressed. Which one? Underline the stressed syllable.

- exercise
- medicine
- physical

- important
- example
- tradition

J Listen and practise saying the words. Decide if the first or second syllable is stressed. Underline the stressed syllable.

1 addiction   8 arthritis
2 enemy   9 personal
3 interested   10 surgery
4 satisfied   11 depression
5 allergy   12 energy
6 natural   13 infection
7 successful   14 prevention

K Using the words and phrases above, write a dialogue between two friends. Student A should describe in detail a health problem that needs attention. Student B should give some tips, using gerunds. Perform your dialogue for the class and decide which best dialogue is. Remember to use the correct stress.

■ EXAMPLE

Student A: I'm feeling terrible. I have a runny nose, a cough and I have aching joints.
Student B: Really? It sounds like you have the flu. How about drinking lots of water?
That can make you feel better ...

A What do you think are the five most serious health problems in the world today?

_____

_____

_____

_____

_____

B Read this article. What health problem does it talk about?

A worldwide epidemic

As of 2005, an estimated 40.3 million people in the world have been diagnosed as living with HIV/AIDS, with sub-Saharan Africa containing the greatest number of cases: approximately 25.8 million people. Unfortunately, only about one sixth of the people with AIDS who live in developing countries are receiving the drugs that they need to survive. Providing good healthcare to infected people is a difficult task for the world.

The causes of HIV (Human Immunodeficiency Virus) are clearly defined by the CDC (Centres for Disease Control). It is most commonly transmitted through sexual contact with infected people, the use of contaminated needles (often for drug use), and blood transfusions of infected blood. Children born to mothers infected with HIV also run the risk of having HIV. Over time, the virus damages the immune system so much that the person is considered to have AIDS (Acquired Immunodeficiency Syndrome).

The consequences of this AIDS epidemic are enormous. The body's immune system weakens. Fighting germs becomes more difficult. The infected person can catch other diseases and illnesses more easily. Many children become orphans when their infected parents die. Strains of the virus can resist current medications. Furthermore, the disease is continuing to spread.

The first HIV/AIDS case was identified in the US in 1981, and since then, more than 25 million people have died. In the mid-1990s, the number of people diagnosed with HIV each year reached a peak and then began to decline. Living with HIV/AIDS is not easy; but with continuing research, education, and improved healthcare, the number of new cases should hopefully begin to decrease everywhere in the world.

C Match the words from the article to their definitions.

1	task	☐	☐	a	high point
2	contaminated	☐	☐	b	job
3	immune system	☐	☐	c	a child whose parents have died
4	orphan	☐	☐	d	the part of the body which fights disease
5	peak	☐	☐	e	dirty; unclean

D According to the article, what do the following numbers represent? Discuss your answers with a partner.

40.3 _____

_____

25.8 _____

_____

1/6 _____

_____

1981 _____

_____

25 million _____

_____

E Can you find any sentences with gerunds as the subject in the article?

F Answer the questions below.

1 How is HIV/AIDS transmitted?
2 What are three consequences of the AIDS epidemic?

G Match the health problems to their definitions.

1 diabetes ☐   ☐ a inability to have children
2 heart disease ☐   ☐ b harmful cells that grow out of control
3 joint problems ☐   ☐ c a feeling of hopelessness
4 stroke ☐   ☐ d restriction of proper blood flow to the heart due to arterial blockages
5 infertility ☐   ☐ e inability to regulate sugar levels in your body
6 cancers ☐   ☐ f issues with the areas where your bones meet, such as at your knees, hips and elbows
7 depression ☐   ☐ g brain injury sometimes causing speech and movement problems

H Choose one of the serious health problems facing the world today. What are the causes of this problem? What are the consequences?

Health problem:

Causes	Consequences

Homework

Do some research on the Internet to find out some recent statistics about the health problems you chose. Using the language learnt in this unit, prepare a presentation about your subject. Cover areas such as causes, symptoms, consequences, cures and living with the disease.

Language Practice

A Fill the gaps with an adjective + preposition combination.

1   Anne was very _____ us. She said 'please' and 'thank you'.

2   Roger was _____ the test, so he couldn't sleep last night.

3   Nina is _____ the dark. She screams when you turn the lights off.

4   What's _____ Edna? She looks sick.

5   The doctor was _____ us. He treated us like animals.

6   My mother is _____ her new car. She really enjoys driving it.

7   Eat your carrots! They're _____ you!

8   I'm _____ what you said to me. It wasn't nice.

9   I'm _____ my job. It's not interesting. I do the same thing every day.

10 Jane is _____ alternative medicine. She loves reading books about massage, acupuncture, aromatherapy and other natural therapies.

B Make sentences with the words.

1   Jonathan / always / argue / his mother

   _____

2   Tim / not / be / very interested / basketball

   _____

3   Natasha / enjoy / play / volleyball

   _____

4   quit / bad habit / not / be / easy

   _____

5   learn / English / take / time

   _____

6   you / think / milk / be / good / your health?

   _____

7   Keon / be / worried / his mother

   _____

8   We / agree / you / about that

   _____

C Fill the gaps.

Dear Sir / Madam,

I would like to apply (1) _____ the position of Care Assistant in the Oaks Retirement Community.

I am interested (2) _____ helping the elderly and caring (3) _____ them. I am good (4) _____ listening (5) _____ people, and I enjoy helping people. I am (6) _____ afraid (7) _____ working hard, and I am a quick learner.

Your company has an excellent reputation for its high standard of care. I would love to have the opportunity to work (8) _____ you.

I look forward to hearing from you soon.

Yours faithfully,
Jodi Evans

D Choose an appropriate adjective to fill the gap. More than one answer may be possible.

1 If I have a _____ headache, I usually take painkillers. However, if the
   pain is _____, I usually need to lie down and close my eyes.
2 Is the pain in your chest _____ or _____?
3 Your cough has become _____. Maybe you should consult a doctor.
4 Earlier, I had a migraine, but now the pain is only _____.
5 Your forehead is burning! You must have a _____ fever.

E Fill the gaps.

1 She's afraid _____ snakes.
2 Does she _____ a fever?
3 Eugenia doesn't like me. She's always rude _____ me.
4 Vegetables are good _____ you.
5 Patsy loves listening _____ country music.
6 When you cut yourself, did you _____ stitches?
7 Did you break your ankle or just _____ it?
8 My doctor _____ these pills for my migraines.
9 I only got a _____ from hitting my leg on the table.
10 What is that man famous _____?

F Look at the answers and write questions.
Ask about the underlined parts of the answer.

┌─■ EXAMPLE ─────────────────────────┐
│ *What is she worried about?*   │
│ *She's worried about her health problems.* │
└────────────────────────────────────┘

1 _____?
   I'm interested in <u>acupuncture</u>.

2 _____?
   He's talking about <u>massage</u>.

3 _____?
   Yin and yang are <u>two different kinds of energy</u>.

4 _____?
   I <u>never</u> feel bored with my work.

5 _____?
   He's good <u>at chemistry and physics</u>.

Language Reference

PREPOSITIONS AFTER ADJECTIVES

We can use prepositions such as 'of', 'for', 'with', 'from', 'in', 'to' and 'about' after certain adjectives.

addicted to

angry at / with

angry about

concerned about

excited about

famous for

good at

good for

happy about

happy with

interested in

nervous about

worried about

Following the preposition, we need to use either a noun or a gerund.

I'm interested in alternative medicine.

Nora is afraid of catching a cold.

Acupuncture can be good for treating headaches.

Cedric is pleased with his treatment.

Nora is worried about her health problems.

PREPOSITIONS AFTER VERBS

Likewise, some verbs are also followed by prepositions.

advise against

be used to

believe in

count on

dream of

get used to

insist on

look forward to

object to

plan on

He advised against taking medicine.

He believes in following the doctor's advice.

GERUNDS

A gerund is the '-ing' form of a verb functioning as a noun. We can use a gerund as a subject, as an object, or as a complement in a sentence.

Gerunds as subjects

Spending time with other people is good for your health.

Breaking promises destroys trust.

Listening shows that you care.

Gerunds as objects

He's very good at listening to other people's problems.

Are you nervous about going to the doctor?

Gerunds as complements

Her worst habit is smoking.

My hobby is running.

disaster

After this unit, you should be able to ...

- Talk about disasters and accidents
- Prepare for an emergency
- Use conjunctions of time: 'before', 'during', 'after', 'while' and 'for'
- Use 'some', 'some of', 'most' and 'most of'
- Use the passive voice to write newspaper headlines
- Write a news article

A How quickly can you respond to instructions? Stand up. Your teacher will give you some commands. Listen carefully and act quickly!

B Now it's your turn to give some instructions to your classmates. Start with a simple instruction, then think of something more complicated. How quickly did your classmates react?

EXAMPLES

Stand up!

Stand on one leg!

Turn to the left, then put your right hand on your head and your left hand on your nose!

C In an emergency situation, it is important to know how to get in and out of a building and where any safety equipment is. With a partner, investigate your classroom and your school and draw a map.

Where are the entrance and exit points?

Where are the stairs?

Where should you go for medical equipment?

Where is the nearest fire extinguisher?

Draw a line showing the best way to leave your classroom in an emergency.

Vocabulary and Listening

A Look at the list of natural disasters below and match each one with the correct definition.

1	hurricane	□	□ **a** large ocean wave, caused by an underwater earthquake or eruption
2	tsunami	□	□ **b** a storm with a violent wind that starts at sea, usually in the Caribbean
3	earthquake	□	□ **c** when steam, rock or hot liquid (lava) bursts from a volcano
4	typhoon	□	□ **d** when sea or river levels rise and cover areas of dry land
5	forest fire	□	□ **e** a mass of snow falling down a mountainside
6	mudslide	□	□ **f** a very dangerous fire which burns huge areas of forest quickly
7	avalanche	□	□ **g** when heavy rains make the ground so wet that it begins to move
8	tornado	□	□ **h** a spinning column of air that moves across land at high speeds
9	flood	□	□ **i** a sudden movement of the earth's surface (crust)
10	volcanic eruption	□	□ **j** a severe tropical storm occurring in the Indian or Pacific Ocean

B This map shows where earthquakes commonly occur.

1 Where do most earthquakes occur?
2 Where are the strongest earthquakes? Why?
3 Where are the safest places?
4 Do you have earthquakes in your country?
5 Are you surprised by anything on the map? What?

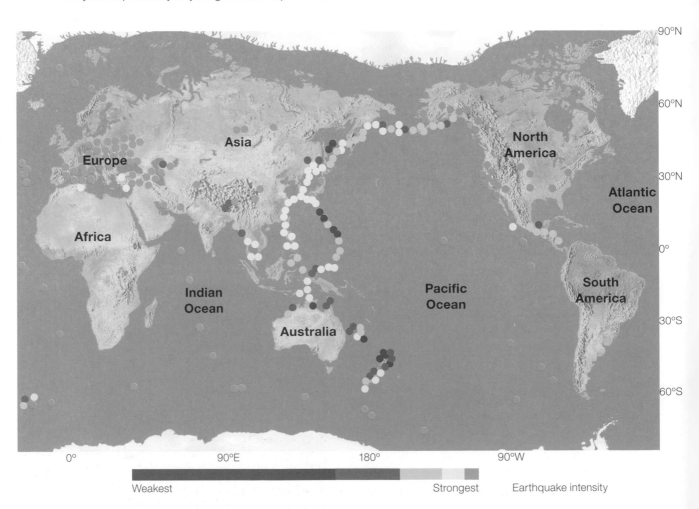

C Answer these questions about natural disasters.

1 What is the difference between a hurricane and a tornado?
2 Which natural disasters do you hear about most often? Can you remember any examples?
3 Which natural disasters most commonly affect your country? What effects do they have?

D Have you ever been in an earthquake? Do you know what to do? Work with a partner to brainstorm ideas for a plan, then make a list with your class. If you have been in an earthquake, share your experience. What did you do during the earthquake? How did you feel while it was happening?

■ **EXAMPLES**

In an earthquake, stand with your back to a strong wall.

If you are inside, don't run out of the house, as something may fall on you.

E Look at the timeline of an earthquake below. Write 'after', 'before' and 'during' in the correct spaces under the timeline.

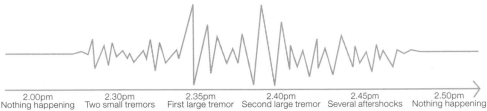

2.00pm	2.30pm	2.35pm	2.40pm	2.45pm	2.50pm
Nothing happening	Two small tremors	First large tremor	Second large tremor	Several aftershocks	Nothing happening

Note: a 'tremor' is a movement of the earth that occurs during an earthquake.

F You are going to listen to an interview about what to do during an earthquake. How closely do your ideas from Exercise D match those you hear?

G Use the chart below to summarise what you should do before, during and after an earthquake.

Before
_____
_____
_____
_____
_____

During
_____
_____

After
_____
_____
_____

H Your teacher will give you the audio script from Exercises F and G. Underline each sentence where 'while', 'during' or 'for' are used to talk about time.

What is the difference in usage between these words? Write the rules here:

- _____ and _____ are used to show that two things happen at the same time.
- _____ is used to show duration of time.
- _____ is used before a subject / verb clause.
- _____ is used before a noun.
- We use _____ before a period of time.

I You are going to play four-in-a-row. To play, take the words provided and create a complete and grammatically correct sentence. Your sentence must contain either 'while', 'during' or 'for'. Try to make four correct sentences in a row.

■ EXAMPLE

the lunch hour
I did my French homework during the lunch hour.

---

the lunch hour	I was on holiday	the class break	we were learning about disasters
a long time	the night	you were sleeping	the thunderstorm
the whole night	a minute	the football match	scientists researched volcanoes
the movie	two weeks	we are taking our exam	the summer

J Do you remember the natural disasters you learnt about? Label each of the pictures below.

1 _____ 2 _____ 3 _____ 4 _____

5 _____ 6 _____ 7 _____ 8 _____

Homework

Look again at your list of natural disasters. You are going to choose one of the disasters and use the Internet to research what to do to prepare for it. Your teacher can help you choose suitable websites. After that, make an action plan for your school. What should you do to prepare before the disaster? What should you do during the event? What should you do afterwards? Do your research thoroughly. You will need this information later in the unit.

Reading and Vocabulary

A What do you know about earthquakes? First, decide if the statements below are True or False. Then read and see if you were right. Correct the statements that are False, based on the reading.

1 **T F** Earthquakes are caused by a build up of pressure in the earth's crust.

2 **T F** It is now possible for scientists to predict an earthquake.

3 **T F** The largest earthquake during the 20th century was in San Francisco in 1906.

4 **T F** Most earthquakes measure between 6.0 and 8.0 points on the Richter scale.

5 **T F** There are over 35 major earthquakes in the world each year.

B Find words or phrases in the text that mean the same as the followings definitions.

1 enormous _____
2 a crack in the earth's surface _____
3 increase _____
4 movements of energy through a substance
_____
5 secondary movements after the earthquake
_____
6 land near the sea _____
7 show, display _____
8 coming before _____
9 the likelihood _____
10 instrument to measure earthquakes _____
11 earthquake scale _____
12 damage (noun) _____
13 causing huge damage and destruction
_____
14 small; unimportant _____
15 discover; find _____

Natural disasters: earthquakes

An ancient Japanese legend tells of a giant catfish that lives underground, causing earthquakes by its restless movements. Earthquakes, needless to say, are not caused by catfish but by a build up of pressure on either side of a fault or crack in the earth's surface. Pressures on the earth's outer layer or crust push the sides of the fault together, causing stress to build up. When the pressure reaches a critical level, the rock suddenly slips, releasing energy in waves that travel through the rock to cause the shaking and tremors that we feel during an earthquake. Secondary shocks, called aftershocks, are often felt for many days afterwards.

While earthquakes themselves can be devastating enough, they often cause additional disasters such as landslides or mudslides, flooding and fire, which increase the damage. If they occur under the sea or near the coast, earthquakes can also cause huge tidal waves–called tsunamis–which can affect countries hundreds or even thousands of miles away. Getting services to those in need can be complicated by power blackouts and damaged roads.

Earthquakes can occur at any time. Although many studies have been made of them, scientists are still unable to predict exactly where or when they may occur. Studies have shown that certain animals and birds exhibit unusual behaviour in the days or weeks preceding an earthquake. Dogs bark, pandas scream, and earthworms and snakes come out from underground in great numbers. Although they cannot predict exactly when an earthquake will occur, scientists can use scientific data to estimate the probability of an earthquake in a particular area. For example, there is a 60-70% chance of a major earthquake in the San Francisco area of the United States by the year 2020.

The size of an earthquake is measured with a seismometer. The largest earthquake of the 20th century occurred in Chile in 1960. It measured 9.5 on the Richter scale. It caused a huge amount of destruction, and the resulting tsunami reached all the way to the Hawaiian Islands, Japan and the Philippines. On December 26th, 2004, an earthquake, which began off the coast of Indonesia and measured a huge 9.0 on the Richter scale, caused the most devastating tsunami in recorded history.

Between 1900 and 1997, an average of 20 major earthquakes each year registered over 7.0 on the Richter scale. However, most earthquakes are much smaller than this. In fact, there are several thousand minor earthquakes every year, which scientists are now able to detect due to the increase in the number of seismographic stations. The data that is collected at these stations is what scientists use to determine the probability of future earthquakes.

Reading and Vocabulary

C Label the map below. Write the correct numbers.

1	the United Kingdom	13	the Arctic
2	the Philippines	14	the Equator
3	the Netherlands	15	the Middle East
4	the Czech Republic	16	the Pacific Ocean
5	the Bahamas	17	the Nile River
6	the People's Republic	18	the Himalayas
	of China	19	the Andes
7	Korea	20	Mount Vesuvius
8	Brazil	21	Lake Victoria
9	South Africa	22	the Mojave Desert
10	New Zealand	23	the Persian Gulf
11	Easter Island	24	the Black Forest
12	Asia	25	the Maldives

D Underline the countries in Exercise C and in the reading passage on page 69. With countries, when do you use the article 'the'? Circle the correct answers and write examples.

1 If a country name is a plural, use / don't use 'the', e.g., _____.

2 If a country name refers to a group of islands (not one island), use / don't use 'the', e.g., _____.

3 If a country name contains words like 'republic', 'kingdom' or 'states', use / don't use 'the', e.g., _____.

4 Simple country names use / don't use 'the', e.g., _____.

E Do these geographical features need 'the' before them? Write '✓' or '✗'.

1	rivers	5	deserts	9	equator
2	oceans	6	gulfs	10	regions
3	mountain peaks	7	lakes	11	forests
4	continents	8	mountain ranges		

Speaking and Listening

A At the end of page 67, you were asked to research how to prepare for a natural disaster. Now you are going to present your findings to the class. First of all, look through your notes and decide how best to present the information. Write notes below.

Introduction: How will you introduce the topic? (Remember to keep this part brief and to the point!)

_____

Before the disaster: What should people do to prepare themselves in advance?

_____

_____

During the disaster: How should people keep themselves safe while the disaster is occurring?

_____

_____

After the disaster: What should people do after the disaster has struck?

_____

_____

Conclusion: Sum up your presentation in a couple of sentences.

_____

B Use these tips to prepare for your presentation.

- Speak; do not read your presentation. It's fine to use notes, but listening to a person speak into a piece of paper is boring.
- Make eye contact and stand up straight.
- Speak slowly, clearly and loudly enough for people to hear you. They want to hear what you have to say!
- Use words that are understandable. If you had to look up a word, your classmates probably don't know it either. Provide useful vocabulary by writing it on the board.
- If possible, use visuals to help your classmates understand.

C Now take time to review and practise your presentation with a partner. Make sure you have everything you need. Remember the tips on how to give a presentation. Practise speaking with your head up.

D Now give your presentation. After you have spoken, ask your classmates for feedback. Take notes on what they liked about your presentation and any suggestions they have on ways to improve future presentations.

E Listen to your classmates' presentations. While you are listening, take notes in your notebook. For each presentation, write, in three columns: 'before', 'during' and 'after'. Write down key words that you hear. Make notes on any new vocabulary that the presenters give you.

F What were two of the most useful or surprising things that you learnt during the presentations?

Speaking and Listening

G Think about the words and phrases that people are likely to use for describing their immediate feelings after witnessing a disaster.

_____
_____
_____

H You are going to listen to four people give first-hand accounts of four disasters. Try to identify which type of disaster each person witnessed.

1 Person 1: _____
2 Person 2: _____
3 Person 3: _____
4 Person 4: _____

I Listen again and answer the questions below.

1 How did the first person feel about what she saw? _____
_____

2 What did the first person do to help?
_____

3 How did the second person survive the disaster? _____

4 How did the third person feel about the disaster she witnessed? _____
_____

5 How did the fourth person react to the disaster he experienced? _____

6 How did the fourth person get to safety?
_____
_____

7 Who reacted well to the situation?
_____
_____

8 Who reacted badly to the situation?
_____

9 Which speakers probably have most experience of natural disasters? _____
_____
_____

10 Which person makes a living from natural disasters? _____

J In a small group, discuss what you would have done in each situation. Did the speaker do the right thing or not? Would you have panicked in the same situation? Take notes on what you would have done differently.

Reading and Speaking

A Have you ever experienced a hurricane or typhoon? What do you know about them? Where do they occur?

B Skim through this news article about a recent hurricane. Where did it take place? How serious was it?

Hurricane Zeus storms into southern Texas

August 1, 2006

CORPUS CHRISTI–Hurricane Zeus made landfall just south of this Texas city onto nearly deserted shores early Monday morning, bringing with it 120 mile per hour winds. The Category 3 hurricane caused flooding along the coast, and widespread blackouts. Numerous trees and street signs were blown down. At least a dozen homes along the coast were severely damaged, one of which was completely washed away in the storm. A mobile home community five miles inland was completely destroyed. Damage is already estimated to be millions of dollars.

Most of the coast surrounding Corpus Christi had been evacuated in preparation for the hurricane. Fearing a direct hit, city officials, over the weekend, ordered a house-to-house mandatory evacuation of those areas that were in most danger. In other communities, those who could not leave in time went to area shelters. Some residents refused to leave, insisting on riding out the storm in their own homes.

So far, three deaths have been reported. A father and his son were killed when a tree landed on their car as they attempted a last minute escape late Sunday night. An elderly woman died of a heart attack. She had refused to leave her home of 87 years.

Flood waters are not expected to begin to recede before Wednesday. Officials have asked people not to come back to the area until the waters return to normal.

C Read the article more carefully, and answer these questions.

1 What size hurricane was Zeus?
2 What are five kinds of physical damage the hurricane caused?
3 How much will it cost to repair the damage?
4 Why were very few people still in Corpus Christi?
5 Why were some people still in the area?
6 How many people died? How did they die?
7 When will people be able to return to the area?

D Match the words from the article to their definition. Which expression can be used idiomatically to mean 'to manage through a difficult situation successfully'?

1 to storm	5 widespread	9 a blackout
2 to make landfall	6 a dozen	10 to be washed away
3 a mobile home community	7 to estimate	11 to evacuate
4 mandatory	8 ride out the storm	12 to recede

a   to go down or go back   b   over a large area   c   to attack suddenly
d   to arrive on land from sea or air   e   a power outage   f   twelve
g   to leave from a place of danger   h   required, must do   i   to wait for bad weather to pass
j   a neighbourhood where all of the homes are light and designed to be transported
k   to give a figure without calculating exactly   l   to be carried to another place by water

Reading and Speaking

 Discuss with a partner.

1 Have you ever been in a blackout? How widespread was it?
2 Have you ever had to evacuate your home?
3 What are some of the pros and cons of living in a mobile home community?
4 Have you ever had to 'ride out a storm'? Was it a real storm, or another type of situation?

F The Saffir-Simpson Hurricane Scale ranks hurricanes on a 5-category scale. Listen and complete the chart below. The first category has been completed already as an example

	Wind speed	Storm surge	Damage	Example hurricanes
Category 1	74-95 mph	4-5 feet above normal	minor	*Hurricane Lili of 2002, and Hurricane Gaston of 2004*
Category 2		6-8 feet above normal		*Hurricane Frances of 2004, and Hurricane Isabel of 2003*
Category 3	111-130 mph		severe	
Category 4				*Hurricane Charlie of 2004, Hurricane Dennis of 2005, Hurricane Wilma of 2005*
Category 5	greater than 155 mph			*Hurricanes, Mitch (1998) and Isabel (2003). Category 5 hurricanes that made landfall include Camille (1969) and Andrew (1992).*

G A hurricane is headed for where you live! Will you evacuate or try to ride out the storm? Share your ideas in a small group, giving reasons for your decision.

H With a partner, role-play the situation below. Imagine that it is currently two days before the hurricane is expected to hit your area. In the end, does Student B decide to stay or go?

Student A
You are a police officer. You have been told to evacuate the entire area. This hurricane is a big one, and it is expected to hit your city directly. If people wait until tomorrow, there may not be time to get everyone out, so they need to go today. Your job is to get people to pack what they absolutely need and get out. There are shelters inland where people can go to be safe.

Student B
You have lived in this town all your life, and you have seen many hurricanes. You have lived through those, and you will live through this one, too. You want to stay in your own home. You need time to board it up first, but you also want to stay to protect it. It could be difficult to get back afterwards. You expect the hurricane to lose strength and speed as it gets near land. Hurricanes often change direction, so your town probably won't get hit directly. Besides, your car is old, and you don't know how far you can drive it.

Speaking and Reading

A The eight pictures below tell a story, but they are in the wrong order. With a partner, try and number the pictures in the correct order.

B You are going to retell the story in the pictures. Here are some words and expressions that may help you. Check your understanding of the words and look up any you don't know in a dictionary.

rope	rescue	fall through the ice	emergency worker	call 999
hole	warn	ice skating	hold onto	break	freezing	treat

C Using the vocabulary from Exercise B, tell the story to your partner. Take turns to talk about each picture.

D Now read this news report about the story. Does it match the order you have?

A local man fell through the ice while he was skating on Long Meadow Pond yesterday. David Shepherd, 34, of Southampton, was skating with his family on the pond at about 3.25pm, when the ice broke beneath him and he fell in. He kept his head out of the water by clinging to the edge of the ice around the hole while his wife called 999 on her mobile.

'I was in the water for about 20 minutes—I couldn't get out,' Shepherd claimed. 'It was freezing.' Four firemen from the Southampton Fire Service arrived at the scene and threw Shepherd a rope. He grabbed it and the firemen pulled him out. He did not suffer hypothermia. Shepherd was flown by helicopter to Southampton General Hospital where he was treated and released.

Police Sergeant Rory Mitchell warned skaters to call their local police station before going out on the ice.

E Answer the following questions.

1 What was Dave Shepherd doing when he fell through the ice? _____

2 Why did he fall in? _____

3 Why did his wife call 999? _____
_____

4 What did he do while he waited for the fire service? _____
_____

5 How long was he in the freezing water?
_____

6 How did the firemen get Dave out of the hole?
_____

7 Was Dave seriously injured? _____
_____

8 The best title for this report would be:
a Ice skating with family is fun and exciting
b Skating on thin ice leads to local rescue
c Skaters should call police before going out

Speaking and Reading

F Look back at the news report. What do these expressions mean?

1 to cling to something _____
2 to grab something _____
3 to suffer something _____
4 hypothermia _____
5 to release someone from something _____

G Your teacher will assign you a role as an eyewitness or as a reporter. Prepare for your interview. If you are an eyewitness, think about how your character would answer the questions in Exercise E.

The eyewitnesses:	The reporters:
• Dave Shepherd	You will interview the different people involved in the skating accident.
• Dave's Wife	
• Fireman	
• Dave's daughter	

H Now, find a partner and act out the role play. Eyewitnesses, remember to speak as that person! Don't simply speak about them.

After a few minutes, rotate partners. Continue until all eyewitnesses have been interviewed by each reporter.

I Now, the reporters should report their findings to the class. Each reporter should tell the class about one of the people he / she interviewed. The rest of the class should listen carefully and take notes.

Homework

For homework, finish your story. Use your notes to write about the other points of view. What kind of order will you use? Will you focus on one eyewitness at a time, or break each story up? Focus on the emotions and experiences of the people who were involved.

J Use your notes from Exercise I to write a human interest story. Human interest stories are different from news articles because they don't just report the facts; they deal with the emotions of the story. Human interest stories are designed to interest and entertain the reader. Focus on the emotions and experiences of the people who were involved.

The first step in writing an entertaining article is to capture the reader's attention with a good introduction. The introduction will get the reader to keep reading. A good introduction has a catchy first sentence.

Write your introduction.

Writing

A Read the headlines. Which is the most eye-catching? Which story would you read first? Which would be the best story to write?

1 EF Student Found Bouncing Off Walls at Local Coffee Shop
2 Favourite Teacher at Local School Buried Under Avalanche of Papers
3 EF Student to Set Record for Continuous Texting
4 EF Student Stuns Teachers by Speaking Only English for Entire Stay
5 School Shocked by Teachers When They Declare 'No Homework Week'
6 EF Student Discovered Labelling Entire School with Flashcards

B Look at these examples of the passive and active voice. Can you say what the difference is?

> **■ EXAMPLES**
>
> *Passive voice:*
> The entire town was destroyed by the earthquake.
>
> *Active voice:*
> The earthquake destroyed the entire town.
>
> *Passive voice:*
> Research on hurricanes will be presented at the conference.
>
> *Active voice:*
> We will present research on hurricanes at the conference.

C

At least a dozen homes along the coast have been severely damaged, one of which was completely washed away in the storm. A mobile home community five miles inland was completely destroyed. Damage is already estimated to be millions of dollars.

There are four examples of the passive voice in this paragraph. Underline each example, and then say how the passive voice is formed.

The passive voice is formed _____

_____.

How would you rewrite these sentences using active voice?

D What kinds of word are taken out of headlines? How would you write each headline from Exercise A as a complete sentence? What tenses do you need? Which sentences use passive voice and which use active?

E In pairs, write the introductory paragraph for one of the headlines. What information should you include?

F You are going to write the rest of the article for your headline. Before you do this, think of some answers to the following questions about your headline.

- Who was involved?
- What happened?
- When did everything happen?
- What did each person do / say?
- Why did it happen?
- What happens next?

Homework

Write the article for your headline. Your teacher will give you a deadline.

Language Practice

A Fill the gaps with 'while', 'during' or 'for'.

1   I hate people who speak _____ they are eating.
2   Did you visit the British Museum _____ you were in London?
3   I hate people who talk _____ a movie.
4   I will stay in the dorm _____ three months.
5   I felt very adventurous _____ my time at university.
6   We mustn't talk _____ the lecture is going on.
7   I woke up four times _____ the night, but my roommate slept solidly
    _____ eight hours.
8   He sleeps _____ the day and works at night.
9   They often have dinner _____ they are watching TV.
10 I talked with my best friend _____ two hours.
11 Let's listen to some music _____ we work.
12 Would you like to go for a drink _____ the intermission?
13 You must not talk _____ examinations are in progress!
14 I usually get a snack _____ the commercials.
15 I have studied karate _____ six years.

B Complete the sentences with the new vocabulary from page 73.

1   After the water _____, we will be able to return to our homes.
2   He lives in a _____ community on the coast.
3   They _____ that it would cost $400 to fix my car.
4   Being out of work for six months was difficult, but I managed to _____.
5   I found _____ of mistakes in your assignment; you will have to do it again.
6   The ocean tide _____ our sand castles.
7   The blizzard last winter caused _____. We had no heat or
    light for two days.
8   Soldiers _____ the castle and quickly gained control of it.
9   Our team captain called a _____ meeting to prepare for our next game.
10 Just after we arrived on the island, we were forced to _____ because the
    volcano was about to erupt.

C Change the following sentences from passive to active voice. (Note: your answers may be slightly different from your classmates'.)

┌─ ■ EXAMPLE ──────────────────────────────┐
│ *The whole village was destroyed by the earthquake.* │
│ *The earthquake destroyed the whole village.* │
└──┘

1   Many homes were damaged in the mudslide.
    _____
2   Experiments on the volcano are being carried out.
    _____
3   The seismometer was invented by Milne.
    _____
4   The sandcastle was swept away by the waves.
    _____
5   Results of the survey will be made available later.
    _____

D Change the following sentences from active to passive voice. You can choose to include the subject or leave it out of the sentence. (Note: your answers may be slightly different from your classmates'.)

> **EXAMPLE**
>
> *Emergency workers helped the tourists to safety.*
> *The tourists were helped to safety by emergency workers.*

1 Thomas Edison invented the light bulb. _____

2 Rivers of mud covered the houses. _____

3 We will conduct more research on earthquakes. _____

4 Researchers have carried out tests on the site. _____

5 Coming back to Tokyo reminds me of the earthquake. _____

E Correct the mistakes in the following sentences and rewrite them.

1 Most the survivors were helped to safety. _____

2 We managed to rescue some the trapped animals from the barn.

_____

3 Some of friends managed to build us a shelter for the night.

_____

4 We saw that most the lights had gone out. _____

5 Reporters told us that some of soldiers had moved into the mountains.

_____

6 Most of school children know what a tsunami is. _____

7 In England, some the people have experienced a hurricane.

_____

8 Some of earthquakes in California are very minor. _____

9 In Kansas, most the people can recognise a tornado. _____

10 Some us are lucky enough never to experience a natural disaster.

_____

F Write six sentences about what you will do before, during and after your next English class.

> **EXAMPLE**
>
> *Before my next class, I will review today's lesson.*

_____
_____
_____
_____
_____
_____

G Correct this list of geographical features. Write ' √ ' if features do not need correcting.

> **EXAMPLE**
>
> *Andaman Islands (incorrect)*
> *the Andaman Islands (correct)*

1 the Lake Erie _____

2 the Sahara Desert _____

3 United States of America _____

4 the Mount Etna _____

5 Panama Canal _____

6 People's Republic of China _____

7 the Equator _____

8 Black Forest _____

Language Reference

CONJUNCTIONS OF TIME: 'WHILE', 'DURING' AND 'FOR'

'While' and 'during' are both used to show that two things happen at the same time.

'For' is used to show duration of time.

What should you do during an earthquake?

Don't run downstairs while the building is shaking.

Earthquakes sometimes last for only a few seconds.

'While' is used before a subject / verb clause.

'During' is used before a noun.

'For' is used before a period of time.

He arrived while I was eating breakfast.

He arrived during breakfast.

He stayed for three hours.

Note: 'for' in 'He arrived for breakfast.' does not show time, but purpose; 'He arrived to eat breakfast.'

USE OF 'THE' WITH GEOGRAPHICAL FEATURES

Countries

We do not usually use 'the' with simple country names, e.g., France, Japan.

But we use 'the' with names which include words like 'republic', 'states', 'union', 'kingdom', e.g., the Czech Republic, the People's Republic of China, the United Kingdom, the United States.

We use 'the' with plural names, e.g., the Netherlands, the Philippines.

These geographical features take 'the':

- rivers: the Amazon
- oceans: the Indian Ocean
- mountain ranges: the Himalayas
- unique geographical features: the Arctic, the Equator
- regions: the Far East, the Middle East
- deserts: the Sahara Desert
- forests: the Black Forest
- gulfs: the Persian Gulf
- island chains: the Marshall Islands, the Bahamas

These geographical features do not take 'the':

- lakes: Lake Baikal
- mountain peaks: Mount Everest
- continents: Europe
- islands (single): Easter Island

PASSIVE VS ACTIVE VOICE

We often use the passive voice in news articles. We use it to emphasise what happened rather than who or what caused things to happen. Compare:

Tremendous damage was caused by the mudslide. (passive voice)

The mudslide caused tremendous damage. (active voice)

We form the passive voice by making the subject of a sentence the object, or by removing the subject altogether.

The earthquake hit Florida. (active voice)

Florida was hit by the earthquake. (passive voice)

We estimate the damage to be extensive. (active voice)

The damage is estimated to be extensive. (passive voice)

Passive sentences often contain the phrase 'by...' to show who or what carried out the action.

Television was invented by John Logie Baird.

The village was stormed by soldiers.

QUANTIFIERS: 'SOME', 'SOME OF', 'MOST' AND 'MOST OF'

'Some' is the plural of 'a', 'an' and 'one'. It is used to talk about indefinite quantities.

I met some interesting people at the party.

There's some coffee in the kitchen.

'Most' is used to talk about the largest indefinite quantities in comparison to others.

In our survey, most people had never experienced a natural disaster.

Most of the coffee has gone.

When we talk generally, we use 'some' and 'most'. 'Some' and 'most' are usually followed by a noun.

Some volcanoes spit out mud and dirt.

Some people didn't make it.

Most people think I'm totally crazy.

When we want to be a little more specific, we use 'some of' and 'most of'. 'Some of' and 'most of' are usually followed by an article.

Some of the local villages were destroyed by the mud.

My father tried to get some of the animals into the barn.

That's why most of the villages beneath Mount Vesuvius got buried by lava all those years ago.

Most of an earthquake's damage is caused in the first few minutes.

values

After this unit, you should be able to ...

- Understand an interview
- Talk about past and present habits
- Use 'used to' correctly
- Pronounce '-ed' endings correctly
- Talk about rhymes and games
- Write a description of a game
- Talk and read about families

A Have you ever played the game 'noughts and crosses'? In North America, this game is called 'tic-tac-toe'. If you don't know the game, ask your teacher to show you.

B Here is a grid for playing noughts and crosses. Play the game with a partner. Who won the game? Why did he or she win?

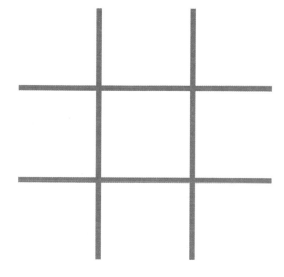

C How would you explain noughts and crosses to someone who had never played it before? Discuss your ideas with a partner and write some instructions.

D Practise saying these tongue twisters to your partner!

- Which witch wished which wicked wish?

- A tree load loved a she-toad
  Who lived up in a tree.
  He was a two-toed tree toad
  But a three-toed toad was she.

Speaking and Listening

A Families and family values have changed a lot in the last forty years. Discuss what you think the definitions of 'family' and 'family values' are. When you have finished, share your ideas with the class.

B Answer the questions about family and family values.

What might be some differences between the following:
- a one-career couple and a two-career couple?
- full-time work and part-time work?
- a single-parent family and a two-parent family?

Name something that is ...
- socially acceptable in your country.
- socially unacceptable in your country.
- good about divorce.
- bad about divorce.

C Read these statements about families. In the appropriate column, put a tick ' ✓ ' next to the statements which you think are true about families in your country today and those which you think were true forty years ago.

	past	present
Two-career couples are common.		
People wait longer to get married.		
There are many mothers working full-time.		
More people choose not to get married.		
Some fathers stay at home to take care of the children and do the housework.		
Many couples choose to live together without getting married.		
There are lots of single-parent families.		
It's not unusual for children to live with their grandparents.		
Divorce is common and socially acceptable.		

D Discuss your choices for each statement. Before you begin your discussion, plan what you are going to say. Make sure you have examples to support your ideas. Use the following phrases when you state your opInions.

In my opinion ...
(Personally) I think ...
I believe that ...
If you ask me, ...

E You are going to listen to Daniel interviewing his father for a school paper. Daniel needs to write an essay for his English class about how things were different for his parents when they were his age. Before you listen, try to predict what kind of things Daniel's father might talk about.

F Listen to the first part of the conversation between Daniel and his father. What is different between life in Daniel's time and life in his father's time? Fill in the table below. Compare your answers with your partner's.

In Dad's time	In Daniel's time (now)
Dad had hair	Dad has no hair
Dad spoke to his father with respect.	
Dad watched TV.	
Dad listened to a Walkman.	
Mothers stayed at home more.	
Fathers worked to support their family.	

G Now listen to the second part of the conversation between Daniel and his father. Fill the gaps in the conversation.

Dad: We (1) _____ use to (2) _____ all the things you do now to entertain us, either. We (3) _____ to find other things to amuse ourselves with.

Daniel: What things (4) _____ you use to (5) _____ with?

Dad: We (6) _____ play with our friends outside, for example. Today, most kids are literally (7) _____ something somewhere indoors. Going to the cinema used to (8) _____ considered going out. Now we have DVDs. And let's not forget what happened to music.

Daniel: What?

Dad: Well, it actually used to be music. Not the noise you kids listen to today.

Daniel: Yeah? I'll bet Grandpa (9) _____ tell you the same thing.

Dad: Actually, now that I think about it, he also used to complain about how family values were changing. He said that we had no idea what it was to earn money or appreciate the value of a dollar. In his day, he had to help support his family. He did lots of chores around the house and (10) _____ to take care of his brothers and sisters. And if he (11) _____ pocket-money, he had to work at a job after school. He (12) _____ that, when he was my age, Walkmans were radios and televisions were called books. He also used to tell me that I spent too much time in front of the TV screen.

Daniel: Like you tell me about the computer screen.

Dad: Yeah. I suppose you're right. I guess some things never change.

H Match the expressions from the conversation between Daniel and his father to their meaning.

1	literally	☐	☐ a	a minor domestic job or task
2	nowadays	☐	☐ b	I'm quite certain.
3	pocket-money	☐	☐ c	I'm paying careful attention.
4	be plugged into	☐	☐ d	in the present period of time
5	chore	☐	☐ e	to be attached to something electronic
6	role	☐	☐ f	following the exact words
7	I'm all ears.	☐	☐ g	It's not important.
8	It doesn't matter.	☐	☐ h	allowance or spending money
9	In my day ...	☐	☐ i	In the time when I was young ...
10	I'll bet ...	☐	☐ j	a person's job, position or function

Grammar and Pronunciation

A Read the audio script from Exercise G on page 83 again. How does Daniel's father talk about the differences between the past and present? Complete the rules.

We use _____ to talk about a situation or habit in the past that doesn't exist in the _____.
We form questions with _____ + subject + _____ + base _____.
We form positive statements with subject + _____ + base _____.
We form negative statements with subject + _____ not + _____ + base _____.

B Write an example of each from the conversation on page 83.

Past habit: _____
Question: _____
Negative: _____

C Rewrite the sentences using 'used to'.

┌─ ■ EXAMPLE ─────────────────────────┐
│ *I lived in Miami in 1994. Now I live in Boston.* │
│ *I used to live in Miami but now I live in Boston.* │
└──────────────────────────────────────┘

1 Brian hated olives when he was a child. Now he loves them.
2 Janice had a lot of bad luck. Now her luck has changed.
3 Did Jake play football when he was at school?
4 Tina wasn't afraid of cats when she was a child.
5 When Katie was younger, she ate a lot of peanuts.
6 Did Maria and Tom live in Mexico before they moved to Costa Rica?
7 Gina loved talking on the phone when she was a teenager.
8 Leo smoked when he was a bartender.

D In a group, look at the table you completed in Exercise F on page 83. Compare how things were different for Daniel and his father while growing up. Remember to use 'used to' when talking about past habits and situations that are no longer true.

E Here is a riddle. See if you can discover who the person is. Then, in your group, create a similar riddle for the rest of the class to solve.

This person used to be a champion body builder. He used to act. He used to live in Austria. He didn't use to speak English. Now, he speaks English, lives in the United States and is the Governor of California. Who is he?

F Work in your group. Ask and answer these questions.

1 Are there any foods you used to eat that you don't eat now?
2 Is there a food you like now that you used to hate?
3 Can you think of something fun you used to do that you don't do now?
4 Is there anything you used to have that you wish you still had now?
5 Is there anything you used to be afraid of?
6 Is there anything you're afraid of now that didn't use to frighten you?
7 What did you use to do when you were a child?
8 What things have changed in your daily routine since you've come to EF?

G Look at the pronunciation rules below. Try and fill the gaps. Then listen to the audio to check your answers.

'Used to' is usually pronounced _____.

┌─ ■ EXAMPLES ─────────────────────────┐
They used to travel all the time.
I used to like ice-cream.
└──────────────────────────────────────┘

The final '-ed' of the simple past of regular verbs can be pronounced in different ways.

After voiceless sounds, the final '-ed' is pronounced _____.

┌─ ■ EXAMPLES ─────────────────────────┐
mixed / worked / liked / kissed / promised
pushed / touched / asked / stopped / finished
└──────────────────────────────────────┘

After voiced sounds, the final '-ed' is pronounced

_____.

┌─ ■ EXAMPLES ─────────────────────────┐
used / planned / smiled / loved / sneezed
pleased / dreamed / closed / arrived
└──────────────────────────────────────┘

After _____ and _____, the final '-ed' is pronounced _____.

┌─ ■ EXAMPLES ─────────────────────────┐
wanted / waited / needed / counted
dated / avoided / hated / traded
└──────────────────────────────────────┘

H Listen to the words. Write them under the correct sounds.

┌──────────────────────────────────────┐
cleaned / cooked / decided / heated / invited
lifted / listened / lived / pulled / shopped
talked / thanked / tried / visited / watched
└──────────────────────────────────────┘

        / t /   / d /

I Look at the sentences. Mark how the '-ed' endings should be pronounced. Listen and check.

1 Denise mixed the ingredients in a bowl.
2 Max used the last light bulb.
3 Jeffrey hated golf, so he played tennis instead.
4 The baby kissed his mother and smiled.
5 William watched videos and listened to music at the same time.
6 The little boy pulled and pushed his train around the room.
7 I really needed that vacation.
8 Sal and Sid finally decided to get married.
9 Marina stopped eating cake and started eating fruit.
10 She was pleased that she dreamed about him.

J On your own, think of more regular verbs in the simple past. Now read them to a partner who should try to decide whether the '-ed' ending is pronounced / t /, / d / or / ɪd /. Did you both agree?

Homework

Use the questions in Exercise F and interview someone from outside the classroom. Write an essay about how the person's life has changed from when they were younger.

        / ɪd /

Grammar and Writing

A Look at the pictures. What is happening? What is the problem? What advice could you give? Here are some different structures used when people give advice. Use them in your answers.

not much food in the fridge

late for work

worried about her friend's health

exams next week

girlfriend's birthday

got a headache

- You should / You should not (shouldn't) ...
- You ought to ...
- You had better (You'd better) / You'd better not ...

1 _____
2 _____
3 _____
4 _____
5 _____
6 _____

B Match the problems on the left with the advice on the right. Then match the completed dialogues with the correct pictures in Exercise A.

1 'There's nothing to eat. Let's go to the supermarket.' ☐

2 'I'm sorry. My car wouldn't start.' ☐

3 'My head's been hurting all week.' ☐

4 'I've got a really important exam next week.' ☐

5 'It's my girlfriend's birthday next week. What should I buy her?' ☐

6 'Have you noticed how tired Chloe's been, lately?' ☐

☐ a 'You should ask her sister. She might have a good idea.' _____

☐ b 'You really shouldn't stay out late this weekend.' _____

☐ c 'I know! She really ought to see a doctor.' _____

☐ d 'This is the third time this week. You'd better not be late again!' _____

☐ e 'OK. But we should make a list before we go.' _____

☐ f 'You'd better get some rest!' _____

C Look at Exercise B and complete the grammar rules below.

We use 'ought to' and 'should' to give _____.
'Ought to' and 'should' are _____ in use. They are both used to express a speaker's _____.

We use _____ for _____ and _____ statements. We use this form for very _____ advice, when we think something negative could happen if the advice isn't taken.

D Make sentences using the prompts.

1 He's got a bad cough. (should / stop smoking) _____
2 It's a really good film. (ought / go and see) _____
3 It's raining. (had better / take an umbrella) _____
4 She rides a motorcycle to work. (ought / wear a helmet) _____
5 You don't look very well. (had better not / go to school) _____
6 Dad is very tired. (should not / drive) _____
7 Sue's really nice. (should / invite her to our party) _____
8 I'm in a hurry. I am already late. (had better / go) _____

E Imagine you haven't arrived at EF, yet. There are many things you might want to know before going to a new school. Write some questions for a student who is at the same school you are going to. What can you ask him or her about? Here are some ideas.

food / classes / entertainment / people / teachers

F Do a role-play using the questions you wrote in Exercise E. Student A hasn't arrived at EF yet. Student B is a student already at the school. They are talking on the phone. Student A is asking questions about the school. Student B is offering advice. Remember to use the expressions you have learnt for offering advice. Swap roles.

> **EXAMPLE**
> *Student A: What are the classes like?*
> *Student B: They're great! The teachers are really friendly and helpful.*

G On a separate sheet of paper, write down an interesting problem you need advice on. If you can't think of one, create one. Pass your paper to every student in the class. Each student should write advice for each problem. Once you have read the advice given, discuss with the class which piece of advice you thought was the best, and why. Remember to use the structures you have learnt for giving advice.

Pronunciation and Writing

A Nursery rhymes are taught to children. They may look like nonsense but they help children to practise the different sounds of English. They also tell stories about events and situations in the past. They can be an interesting look at a country's history.
Look at these old nursery rhymes and try to match them to their possible history.

a   Three blind mice, three blind mice.
    See how they run, see how they run.
    They all ran after the farmer's wife,
    Who cut off their tails with a carving knife.
    Did you ever see such a thing in your life
    As three blind mice?

b   Hey, diddle diddle,
    The cat and the fiddle,
    The cow jumped over the moon.
    The little dog laughed

To see such fun,
And the dish ran away with the spoon.

c   The grand old Duke of York,
    He had ten thousand men,
    He marched them up to the top of the hill
    And he marched them down again.
    When they were up, they were up.
    And when they were down, they were down.
    And when they were only half-way up,
    They were neither up nor down.

1   This rhyme is about the daughter of Henry VIII. Queen Mary I, or 'Bloody Mary' as she was known, was a very devout Catholic who treated Protestants very badly. Once, three noblemen tried to kill her, but were caught and killed. _____

2   One story is that this rhyme is about pub crawl in the United Kingdom. A pub crawl is when people go to as many pubs in one night as they can. The pubs, 'The Cat and the Fiddle' etc, were actually real. They were built in the early 1700s, about six miles apart from each other. Some of them still exist. _____

3   Most believe that this nursery rhyme is about wars called 'The Wars of the Roses'. The wars lasted thirty years between the House of Lancaster, whose symbol was a red rose, and the House of York, whose symbol was a white rose. _____

B Do you have any nursery rhymes in your country? If you can think of one, share it with the class. Say it in your own language, and explain what it means in English.

C Listen to some words from Exercise A. Complete the table with more rhyming words from the nursery rhymes. One word doesn't have any rhyming words.

Sound	Examples	Rhyming words
/ e/	ten	
/ aɪ /	mice	
/ ɪ /	fiddle	
/ u: /	moon	
/ ɑ: /	farmer	
/ ʌ /	cut	

D Now practise saying the nursery rhymes with the correct pronunciation of the rhyming words.

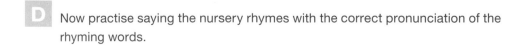

E Listen and circle the word that rhymes with the word you hear.

1 seat / fit / sight
2 look / clock / luck
3 moose / mice / house
4 pen / Jenny / pay
5 cable / tablet / taboo
6 foot / fold / rude
7 chose / toes / whose
8 sunny / morning / Monday
9 dad / grade / glass
10 cop / pup / cub

F Using the words in Exercises C and E, or other words of your own, write a nursery rhyme that might show future people about our history. Here are some ideas of things to write about.

technology	fast food	the Internet
world affairs	sports	

G Children's games are another way we can learn about a country's culture. Here are the names of three games from the UK. Working with a partner, discuss what you think might happen in these games. Don't read the descriptions yet!

garden hopping	pillow fight	knock and run

Now try to match these games with the descriptions below.

In Britain, some children love to play games that are risky and are actually quite anti-social.

Game 1: _____ Children select a house, often somewhere where somebody scary lives! They then go up and knock on the door, and try to get away as fast as they can before the person arrives at the door!

Game 2: _____ This is a game that takes place on long streets with lots of houses with back gardens. A group of children will climb over the fence to a garden at one end of the street, then they try to climb over fences into as many gardens as they can without getting caught!

Game 3: _____ This is a crazy game played at parties (without the parents knowing) in which all the children get in one room—normally the children's bedroom. Then they turn off the lights and have a big play fight in the dark with pillows!

H Here are some other popular children's games. Try to match the pictures to the name of the game.

hide-and-seek	hopscotch	dodge ball	tag
☐	☐	☐	☐
☐	☐	☐	☐

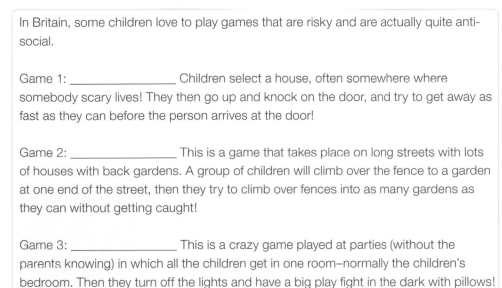

Homework

Write a short article about children's games in your country. Bring your article to the next lesson to show your classmates. Remember to describe how each game is played.

Reading and Listening

A What usually happened when you got home from school when you were younger? Were your parents there when you got home? Were they cooking dinner? Could you play or did you have to do your homework first? Remember to use 'used to' when answering the questions!

B The text below is about 'latchkey kids'. What do you think the expression means? Read the text and find out if your guess was correct.

In the United States, almost half of all young elementary school children are left alone at home at some time during the day. These children are called 'latchkey kids'. Their numbers are increasing due to the rising numbers of single-parent and two-career families. Latchkey kids come home after school and take care of themselves. The house key is often hidden in a secret place. That's how latchkey kids get their name. 'We hide the key in the dog house,' says eight-year old Brian.

Does it cause problems for the child? That depends. Many psychologists strongly believe that children under nine years old should not be left by themselves. Others believe that some children do well when they're on their own and that self-care can be a positive experience for them. They enjoy having the time to do their homework or to work on their hobbies.

It's clear that being a latchkey kid can be difficult for many children. There are hotlines set up around the country for unsupervised children to call. Children call the hotlines because they are bored, lonely or scared. Some children are asked to supervise their younger brothers or sisters. That's a big responsibility, and the situation can make all of the children in the house feel anxious and unsafe.

What do latchkey kids do when they feel insecure? The number one solution is television. TV is seen by the children as company. It breaks the silence in the house and covers up scary noises. Pets help, too. 'When I feel lonely, I just talk to our dog, Barney,' Brian explains. 'We play games, and he helps the time go faster.' Brian's mother works over 100 hours a week in low-paying jobs so that Brian can have a nice home in a middle-class neighbourhood. 'I want Brian to live in a safe neighbourhood and to go to a good school. I work these long hours for him.'

C Are the statements True or False?

1 **T F** The number of latchkey kids is growing.
2 **T F** Latchkey kids were named after a psychologist.
3 **T F** Everyone agrees that children under nine years old shouldn't be left alone.
4 **T F** Being alone after school can be a positive experience for some children.
5 **T F** When a child is unsupervised, there is usually a parent somewhere nearby.
6 **T F** A child might call a hotline for unsupervised children if he or she is bored.
7 **T F** Latchkey kids often watch TV when they feel lonely or afraid.

D Find the word / words in the text that mean the following.

1 look after _____

2 to put in safe place only you know about _____

3 by one's self _____

4 a telephone service to help people with personal problems _____

5 to be in charge of looking after someone or something _____

6 being uneasy about certain events or matters _____

7 not certain; to have doubts; unsafe _____

8 to belong to the part of society that is between the upper and lower classes _____

E Brian's mother works very long hours so that Brian can live in a nicer home and go to a better school. As a result, Brian spends many hours at home alone. Work with a partner and discuss the following questions.

1 Is Brian's mother right?

2 Is the situation hurting Brian more than it's helping him?

3 What do you think is the best thing about being a latchkey kid? What's the worst thing?

4 How might life be different for you today if you had / hadn't been a latchkey kid growing up?

F There is a lot of stereotyping of single mothers. Now discuss what you imagine the stereotypical single father is like.

G Discuss these questions with your partner.

1 Are single parent families common in your country?

2 Are they socially acceptable?

3 Do the courts in your country prefer to give custody to mothers or fathers when parents divorce?

4 In your opinion, are single mothers better than single fathers? Why?

5 Are there things that only a mother / father can give her / his children?

6 What are some of the advantages / disadvantages of coming from a single-parent family?

H You are going to listen to an interview with a single dad and his son. What questions would you ask if you were doing the interview? Listen and see how many of your questions are answered.

I These are some common expressions that Nick's dad uses in the interview. In what situations can you use them?

It's our pleasure. _____

There aren't enough hours in the day.

_____

I'm never more than a phone call away.

_____

I don't know what I'd do without him.

_____

I shouldn't have told you that. _____

His specialty is ... _____

Homework

Write a couple of paragraphs about a typical day in your life when you were a child.

Je are doing   We will d

Reading and Speaking

A Unfortunately, not all families are happy ones. Many families today are considered to be dysfunctional. What do you think this word means?

B Here are some problems common to families that are dysfunctional. Write down some other possible problems.

- mental illness
- an addiction to drugs or alcohol

_____

_____

_____

_____

_____

_____

D Read the article and answer the questions.

1 What phrase in the first paragraph means: 'All the people have the same opinion'?
2 According to the article, what four things do 'normal' and 'dysfunctional' families have in common?
3 Can you give an example of someone going through 'hard times'?
4 What does the article mean by 'negative attention'?
5 Can you describe a person going through a 'mood swing'?
6 What other words can you collocate with 'develop'?

> ■ EXAMPLES
> _develop friendships / develop an idea_

7 Name two skills you lack, that you would like to develop.
8 What other things can 'show up unexpectedly', that annoy you?

C You are going to read an article about dysfunctional families. Before you read the article, look up these words in a dictionary. These words will help you understand the text better.

misbehaviour	conflict
abuse	ignored
participate	sense
exposed	mood swings
lack	form

'Dysfunctional families' is a term that has been used a lot over the past years. It's used so often that sometimes it's hard to understand exactly what it means. For the most part, it is agreed that a dysfunctional family is one where misbehaviour, conflict and even abuse can happen on a regular basis. These behaviours are usually caused by certain members of the family. Children growing up in families of this kind can often think that living this way is normal. Of course, there is no such thing as a perfect family. All families argue, hurt each other's feelings, experience sadness and go through hard times. However, this is very different from being part of a dysfunctional family.

There's a good chance that you know someone who comes from a home that is far from perfect. Perhaps a brother or sister feels so ignored that they participate in socially unacceptable activities in order to get attention—even if it is only negative attention. Maybe the mother is an alcoholic. Or maybe the father screams without warning because of something as simple as a broken dish. These could all grow into long-term problems for the family as a whole, as well as for each individual member.

Take Maude, for example. Maude had to grow up in a home where she was constantly exposed to her father's sudden and scary mood swings. She's a good student, without many friends. And although there's nothing 'unusual' about her, her classmates still sense that she is unhappy. Her father's mental illness, in addition to the dysfunctional home environment, prevents Maude from developing close and intimate friendships. She simply lacks the social skills needed to form such relationships.

Maude is not the only one, either. A lot of people go off to college, have careers, are in relationships and see the effects of what they experienced only later on in life. And, as much as they'd like to leave this part of their life behind, it has a strange way of showing up unexpectedly.

E Imagine you are having a conversation on the 'Family Crisis Hotline'. Student A is a hotline phone counsellor and Student B is a person with the following problem. Create a dialogue with your partner to share with the class.

> Student A: Don't forget to use the appropriate language when giving advice!

> Student B: You are a thirteen-year-old. Your sixteen-year-old brother is a cruel person. He is often very mean to you. Your parents both work, so they are hardly around. Your brother is the 'perfect child' when they are home and your parents don't believe you when you say that he is mistreating you. Lately, it's become worse. You are starting to get scared that he may physically hurt you. You've decided to call the 'Family Crisis Hotline'.

F How much of this family tree can you fill in? Tell your partner about your family. Ask questions about his / her family.
Here is some vocabulary to help you.

great-great-grandmother / great-grandfather / grandfather / grandmother
mother (mum / mom) / father (dad) / brother / sister / step (half) brother, mother, etc.
aunt / uncle / cousin / niece / nephew / mother in law / brother-in-law /
on my father's / mother's side

Information about grandparents

Information about parents and aunties and uncles

Information about your siblings and cousins

|
me

G Think of an interesting story about one of your relatives to tell the class.

Language Practice

A Match the halves to make complete sentences.

1 She used to be afraid of snakes, ☐   ☐ a but now he's in jail.
2 They used to travel a lot, ☐   ☐ b but now she won't eat them.
3 He used to be rich, ☐   ☐ c but now he's a single dad.
4 Darren used to like Vicky, ☐   ☐ d but now they have children.
5 Bob used to rob banks, ☐   ☐ e but now she uses the lift.
6 A mouse used to live in the kitchen, ☐   ☐ f but now she has a pet snake.
7 James used to come home after school, ☐ ☐ g but now he lives in an old basement.
8 Fiona used to love cucumbers, ☐   ☐ h but now he's in love with Betty.
9 Steven used to be married, ☐   ☐ i but now he goes to his dad's office.
10 Patricia used to take the stairs, ☐   ☐ j but now the cat sleeps in there.

B Rewrite the following sentences with 'used to'.

1 When Lin was at elementary school, he read a lot of books.

   _____

2 Maria lived by the beach for several years.

   _____

3 A spider lived in our bathroom for six months.

   _____

4 Bruce and Alan went to the movies every week when they were in college.

   _____

5 Did you have a lot of bad dreams when you were a child?

   _____

6 She didn't drink milk when she was a child, but now she does.

   _____

7 Doris was a famous actress before she became an accountant.

   _____

8 Sam smoked more than twenty cigarettes a day when he was a teenager.

   _____

C Find the mistake in each sentence and correct it.

1 You shouldn't to give babies too much sugar.

   _____

2 I use to smoke cigarettes.

   _____

3 They ought to better wait for the bus.

   _____

4 Teresa used to drank a lot of beer.

   _____

5 Should mothers working full-time?

   _____

6 Children shouldn't to be alone.

   _____

7 She had better to learn to speak English.

   _____

8 Millie should not to talking during the test.

   _____

D Here are some popular games. Choose one and write a description of how it is played. You may also choose a game of your own to write about.

> Monopoly, Snakes and Ladders, hopscotch, chess, Go, Sudoku, Chinese chess, snooker, hide-and-seek, Trivial Pursuit, tag

■ EXAMPLE

To play Snakes and Ladders, you need a board, a dice and some counters.
First, you should throw a dice and move your counter along the board.
If you land on a ladder, you have to climb the ladder…

_____

_____

_____

_____

_____

_____

_____

E Practise pronouncing the following words and sentences correctly. Pay attention to your pronunciation of the past tense verb endings.

- finished
- ended
- exterminated
- bothered
- jumped
- emptied
- landed
- lifted
- camped

1 Carrie wasn't bothered when the cat jumped on her.
2 After the plane landed, we all jumped in a taxi.
3 When the school term ended, we went to the countryside and camped near a lake.

F Look at the list of habits below. Complete the table with sentences about what you do now and what you used to do in the past. The first examples have been done for you.

> brush my teeth, go swimming, travel to school, learn English, choose my clothes, cook my meals, tie my shoelaces, drive a car, do my homework, talk to my parents

In the past	Now
My mother used to help me brush my teeth.	Now I brush my teeth myself.
I used to go swimming once a week.	Now I go swimming every day.

Language Reference

'USED TO'

We use 'used to' to talk about a situation or habit in the past that doesn't exist in the present.

> *Janet used to live in Ireland. Now she lives in Singapore.*
> *Erica used to go out with her friends. Now she stays at home with her baby.*
> *Lorenzo used to work for a major corporation. Now he's self-employed.*

We form questions and negatives with 'did' and 'use to'.

> *Did you use to have red hair?*
> *Did Tim use to play the trombone?*
> *I didn't use to like her.*
> *She didn't use to spend so much money.*

When we use 'used to', we usually contrast the past situation with the present one.

> *Junk food used to be more popular. Nowadays, people eat healthier meals.*

GIVING ADVICE

'Ought to', 'should / shouldn't' and 'You'd better (not)…' are all used to give advice. 'Ought to' and 'should' are very similar in use. They are used to give the speaker's opinion.

> *You should try turning it off and on again.*
> *You ought to try to avoid working too much.*

'Had better' behaves differently from 'should' and 'ought to'. It is used for urgent advice.

> *You had better go to the police station right away!*

PRONUNCIATION OF '-ED' IN PAST TENSE OF REGULAR VERBS

The final '-ed' of the simple past of regular verbs can be pronounced in different ways.

After voiceless sounds, the final '-ed' is pronounced / t /.

> *mixed / worked / liked / kissed / promised / pushed / touched / asked / stopped / finished*

After voiced sounds, the final '-ed' is pronounced / d /.

> *used / planned / smiled / loved / sneezed / pleased / dreamed / closed / arrived*

After 't' and 'd', the final '-ed' is pronounced / ɪd /.

> *wanted / waited / needed / counted / dated / avoided / hated / traded*

behaviour

After this unit, you should be able to ...

- Use infinitives with adjectives
- Talk about manners
- Listen to a radio show
- Read about email manners
- Read about culture shock
- Write and make a presentation
- Write a report

A Are you good at giving compliments? Stand up and talk to each of your classmates. You must pay each person in the room a different compliment before you sit down again.

B Stand up again. Use the phrases below to find someone in your class who ...

- hates writing emails
- thinks spitting in the street is rude
- thinks spitting in the street is OK
- knows what a 'taboo' is
- loves living in a new culture
- hates living in a new culture
- makes friends easily
- enjoys arguing with people online
- thinks good manners are very important
- thinks good manners are unimportant

C Brainstorm some examples of good manners and bad manners. Think about manners at home, at work, at school, when eating at a restaurant, when talking to elderly people and when on vacation. Write some ideas below.

Good manners:

Bad manners:

Reading and Speaking

A Think about two countries you have visited or studied. How did manners vary in each place?

B The text below comes from a guidebook for foreigners visiting Moscow. Your teacher will tell you which section to read. Do not look at the other sections. When you have finished, find people in the class who read the other sections. Swap information with them and write notes.

1 Presents

When visiting a Russian friend's house for dinner, it's important to make sure you bring flowers or chocolates as a present. If you are buying flowers, check that there is an odd number—an even number of flowers is considered unlucky! When meeting a government official, it is wise to bring a small present as a sign of respect. It can be difficult to do business in Moscow without some local connections.

2 Visiting

Russians are happy to invite new friends to their home, rather than meeting in a restaurant or pub. When you visit somebody's home, it is polite to take off your shoes. If you come for dinner, don't be hesitant to bring a gift such as a bottle of wine, or a bottle of vodka. It is traditional to drink vodka, especially when giving a toast. Don't bring warm vodka to a party. Be careful to keep it in the freezer before drinking.

3 Language

English speakers show enthusiasm or interest by a rising intonation at the end of a sentence. But Russian people can sometimes show enthusiasm by doing exactly the opposite! Although many people in Moscow speak English, it is good to learn some Russian words and phrases in advance. Russians are not as likely to use words like 'great' or 'brilliant' in conversation, either. This means that foreigners who constantly use these words might sound a little false to Russians.

4 Transport

On the Moscow underground, Russian people sit or stand quietly and read novels or newspapers. It is rude to hold a loud conversation with a friend. Be careful to follow this rule—it can be difficult for people from 'louder' countries to understand how annoying they seem to the quiet passengers!

Bus queues in Moscow can be a little crazy. Be ready to hold your ground! Personal space in Russia is slightly less than in most English-speaking countries. However, Russians do not like being touched by strangers. If you need to get through a crowd of people, be prepared to use your body rather than your hands to push through.

5 Smiling and Laughing

Russians can often seem reserved and unsmiling in public. It is unwise to expect a shopkeeper to smile automatically when serving you. This is not because Russians are unfriendly. Instead, they are aware that life can be hard sometimes. Smiling all the time seems unnecessary. It's important to get used to this. Try to be yourself with your Russian friends, but it's sensible to avoid 'false' laughter and smiles. Russians have a saying, 'Laughter for no good reason is the hallmark of a fool.' Russians are content to keep smiles and laughter for social occasions and happy events.

6 Clothing and Posture

In Russia, it is very impolite to put your coat on the back of your chair in a restaurant. You should remember to give your coat to the wardrobe attendant, or you will seem cheap. Especially when going out, Russians would be ashamed to be seen in casual clothes. It is wise to follow their example. Be sure not to stand with your hands in your pockets or with folded arms when talking to an older person. Finally, don't slouch in your chair and don't cross your legs with one ankle resting on your knee. Showing the soles of your feet is considered rude.

C Now read the rest of the text to check if your notes were correct.

D Work with a partner and answer the questions below.

1 What word or phrase in the 'Presents' fact file means:
a numbers like 1, 3, 5, 7 _____
b smart, intelligent _____
c a feeling of admiration and esteem for a person and their achievements _____

2 What word or phrase in the 'Visiting' fact file means:
a cautious _____
b a fridge that keeps food below 0°C _____

3 What word or phrase in the 'Language' fact file means:
a a feeling of great excitement and interest

_____
b beforehand _____
c not real or genuine _____

4 What word or phrase in the 'Transport' fact file means:
a causing irritation or trouble _____
b the private individual space around a person

_____
c to believe in something strongly and not move from your position (physically or mentally)

_____

5 What word or phrase in the 'Smiling and Laughing' fact file means:
a doing something without thinking about it; unconsciously _____
b become accustomed to something _____
c a distinguishing feature _____

6 What word or phrase in the 'Clothing and Posture' fact file means:
a reluctant to spend money _____
b to sit or stand in a way which is overly relaxed and informal _____

E What stereotypes do you think people have about your nationality? Write down your ideas.

F Now test your ideas. Interview other students in your class. Do they agree with your ideas? Put a tick ' √ ' next to stereotypes they agree with, and a cross ' X ' next to stereotypes they disagree with.

G Discuss the following questions.

1 Why do we have stereotypes?
_____
_____

2 Can a stereotype be completely true or completely false?
_____
_____

3 Are stereotypes useful? How?
_____

4 Are there any ways in which stereotypes can be dangerous? How?
_____

5 Do stereotypes about your country make you feel uncomfortable? Why or why not?
_____
_____

H Think of ten questions to ask other people about stereotypes of their country and nationality.

> ■ EXAMPLE
> *What stereotypes do you think other people have about your country?*

Homework

Use your questions to survey people outside of your class. Interview five people and save the information for later in the week. You will need it to help you make a presentation.

Grammar and Listening

A Mix and match the words from below to write some sentences about good and bad manners around the world. (Note: there are many possible combinations.)

1	~~afraid to~~ ☐	☐ a	put	In England, people are often afraid to admit when they are angry.
2	impolite to ☐	☐ b	invite	_____
3	polite to ☐	☐ c	use	_____
4	rude to ☐	☐ d	drink	_____
5	wise to ☐	☐ e	hold	_____
6	hesitant to ☐	☐ f	follow	_____
7	happy to ☐	☐ g	take off	_____
8	ashamed to ☐	☐ h	ignore	_____
9	prepared to ☐	☐ i	~~admit~~	_____
10	ready to ☐	☐ j	do	_____
11	careful to ☐	☐ k	eat	_____
12	likely to ☐	☐ l	bring	_____

B Look at Exercise A and complete the rule.

We often use a form of the verb _____
+ an _____ + an _____ to
describe feelings, attitudes and customs.

C Look back at the fact files about Russia. You will find many sentences containing an adjective + infinitive combination. Underline all the examples you can find.

Look at the fact file on 'Smiling and Laughing'. Can you find the phrase containing 'used to'? Can you see that 'used to' is used differently from phrases like 'polite to' and 'likely to'?

D You are going to listen to a radio phone-in show with Marla Stewart, an expert on manners. You will listen to Harvey ask Marla for advice about a dinner party he is going to give. What things might you ask about if you were calling?

E Now listen to the radio show. Did you have some of the same ideas?

F Now listen again and fill the gaps using the structure you learnt in Exercise A.

1 I'm _____ and _____ you with all your questions about proper manners.
2 Harvey has a few queries about what a good host is _____.
3 My parents were _____ me how important they can be.
4 It's _____ your elbows on the table.
5 It's _____ with your mouth full.
6 It's definitely _____.
7 Just remember, it's _____ the toast sincere.
8 When you clink glasses, it is _____ the other person in the eye.
9 Be _____ people.
10 Most people are _____ themselves.
11 Also, be _____ people with common interests next to each other.
12 This way you'll be _____ your party more.
13 Don't be _____ a friend for help.
14 It's _____ your guests that they have overstayed their welcome.

Speaking and Reading

A What do you think this quotation means? Discuss your ideas together with the class.

'It's good to have an end to journey toward, but it's the journey that matters in the end.'

B Most people who move to a new country or place go through 'culture shock'. Culture shock is a condition of confusion that may affect us when we are suddenly exposed to an unfamiliar culture or way of life. Think about your own experience of culture shock. Are you in a new country? Have you ever spent time in an unfamiliar culture or moved to a new city? What are some of the things that shocked you? Note down some of them.

C Think about your current or past experience of any new place. First, interview your partner using the following questionnaire. Then, write four questions of your own connected with 'culture shock' and interview your partner.

1 What do / did you like the most about this place?
2 Is there anything that annoys / annoyed you about this place?
3 How would you describe the people in this place?
4 What did you know about this place before you arrived?
5 Did you know any stereotypes about this place before you arrived?
6 How much did this place differ from what you expected?
7 Were the stereotypes that you knew about before you arrived true or false?
8 Are you glad that you came / went to this place? Why or why not?

9 How much time do / did you spend thinking about your home?
10 What do / did you miss about your home?
11 Who are / were your friends here / there?
12 Do you think you spend / spent too much time with people from your own culture?
13 Are you experiencing / Did you experience 'culture shock'? Can you describe what it feels like?
14 What have you learnt / Did you learn about this place and its people from your experience?
15 What have you learnt / Did you learn about your own home and people from your experience?
16 What will you miss when you return home / What did you miss while you were gone?

D Now talk to as many people from your class as you can. Share your answers from the questionnaire. If you are in a new culture, discuss how culture shock is affecting you now.

Speaking and Reading

E It is common for people experiencing a new culture to go through different stages of culture shock. Think about your own experience or the experiences of your friends. With a partner, discuss what the different stages of culture shock might be. What is the first stage of culture shock? What about after six months or more?

F Read about the four stages of culture shock. Have you experienced any of these stages? Do you agree with the way the stages are described?

1 Honeymoon
Everything seems great and so exciting! You see all the good things and can ignore the bad things, as you may not even be aware of them yet! You can't help grinning a lot when you see new places or traditions!

2 Shock
You become aware of the negative sides of the culture. In fact, it is hard not to focus on them. You miss your own culture, and your own friends and family. You feel uncomfortable, you can get ill easily and you sleep either very little or way too much. You may feel like you want to go home. Language difficulties will frustrate you.

3 Balancing
You focus less on the bad things. You also start to balance your own culture with the new one. You feel pleasure in learning things about the new culture, and start to understand things like the humour of the people. You are more familiar with your new environment. You enjoy your time and feel like you belong, or as if you soon will.

4 Integration
You have a better understanding of both good and bad things about the new culture. You feel comfortable in the new culture and can start to think about your goals and what you can achieve in that culture. You have a more solid feeling of belonging.

G Now answer the following questions.

1 How long have you lived in a new culture / did you spend in a new culture?
2 Have you experienced any of the things described in the four stages?
3 What have you NOT experienced?
4 How much do / did you feel that you belong / belonged in your new culture?

H Look at the graph below. Decide where on the graph the four stages you read about belong.

I Draw a line on the graph to represent your own experience of culture shock, marking the four stages on your line to show if and when you experienced each one.

Happiness

Time

J Read the article about culture shock.

Everybody who experiences a new culture suffers from culture shock to some degree. The first thing is to remember who you are. You are as interesting to your new friends as they are to you, and you have a lot to offer your new culture. Find other people from your own culture so you have some support and familiarity—but don't rely on them too much. After all, this is a unique experience. Take the chance to immerse yourself in the new culture and learn as much as you can.

You will especially need to learn the language, get used to the slang and the speed that native speakers speak. Even people who have studied a language for many years are often shocked at how little they understand at first. But don't worry—the ear is like a muscle; the more you exercise it, the stronger it will get.

Culture shock is a form of stress, so any activity that reduces stress will help—especially plenty of exercise. Find out where you can swim or join a gym—and if you are good at any team sports, try to find out where you can get involved. This will help you to meet new friends with a common interest. If you are not sporty, then think about whether you have any hobbies that will help you to unwind, and to meet people. Another way to lower stress is to simply relax. There will be many things that you want to do and places to explore —but don't forget that sometimes you just need to slow down and take some time to be by yourself.

Don't expect that it will always be easy, but don't be too hard on yourself if you find the experience of adapting to your new culture difficult. Remember that you are not alone in feeling culture shock—it's natural—so allow yourself to feel sad. Of course, you will miss your own culture, especially your family and friends from home. But don't feel bad about feeling bad!

It's important to keep in contact with your friends and family from home. These days, with email and Internet messenger services, and also with the incredibly cheap phone cards that you can buy from any corner store, it is easy to keep in touch with the people you love anywhere in the world.

Take control! If there are things that you don't like about the new culture, then find ways to avoid those things as much as possible, and concentrate on experiencing the things you enjoy and the things that you are interested in.

It's good to have goals. You came to the new country for a reason; so don't lose sight of that reason. Write down your goals. Think about what you want to achieve during your time in the new country and work to achieve those goals. Don't forget them! But don't worry if your goals change or you don't manage to achieve everything you planned. The important thing is to enjoy the moment as much as you can.

K Which paragraphs express the following ideas? Put the number of the appropriate paragraph next to each sentence.

Focus on the events that give you pleasure. _____
You shouldn't depend too much on people with similar backgrounds. _____
Discover the native language and ways of speaking. _____
Have a good time. _____
Put your objectives down on paper and keep them in mind. _____
Don't worry if you don't feel happy. _____
Don't forget that there is a lot you can give others. _____
Keep in contact with family and friends from home. _____
In order to reduce anxiety, try to work out and take it easy. _____

Homework

Use the questionnaire in Exercise C to survey people outside of your class. You may wish to add some more questions of your own. Interview five people and save the information for later in the week. You will use it to help you give a presentation.

Reading and Writing

A   Work with a partner. What do we mean by the word 'taboo'? Can you think of some 'taboos'?

B   Now read the text to check your answer.

What is a taboo? A taboo is something that the society you belong to thinks is offensive, embarrassing or wrong. The word can also be used as an adjective. For example, 'It is taboo to discuss religion in the classroom.' Some taboos are common to all societies. For example, murder is taboo throughout the world. However, some taboos are not shared by everyone.

Taboos are not the same as laws. You can usually break taboos without legal punishment, but doing so may make people uncomfortable. For example, certain swear words are taboo in conversation. At work, it may be taboo for a man not to wear a jacket and tie. For some people, it may be taboo to talk about a person's weight or age.

Note: When we do something that is considered taboo, we 'break' that taboo. For example, if you walk naked down the street in London (and in most other parts of the world) you are breaking a taboo!

C   Work with a partner and answer the questions.

1   How are taboos different from laws?
_____

2   Name some taboos common to all societies.
_____

3   Name some taboos specific to your society.
_____

4   Have you ever broken a taboo? What happened?
_____

5   Name a book or film that explores a taboo. What was the taboo?
_____

6   What generally happens to people who break taboos?
_____

D   Look at these actions. Which ones are considered taboo in your society? Put a tick '✓' in the appropriate box according to your opinion.

	Nobody cares	Slightly rude	A taboo	A very strong taboo
Spitting in the street				
Staring at a stranger				
Coughing without covering your mouth				
Putting your feet up on a table				
Wearing a hat during dinner				
Picking your nose in public				
Smoking in a public place				
Eating food in the street				
Playing your stereo too loudly				
Burping after a good meal				
Kissing in public				
Talking during a film				
Breastfeeding a baby in public				
Laughing during a funeral				
Walking barefoot in a shop				

E Think of five things that people in your society find unacceptable and interview other people in your class.

F Read the sentences below and discuss the meaning of the vocabulary in **bold** with your partner. These words are often used in reports.

In addition to the findings presented in my report, I would like to share with you the results of a survey we conducted last week. **Furthermore**, my colleague, Professor Menzies, will be presenting some new evidence in support of our ideas.
Since we began researching this topic, it has become clear that a much more detailed investigation is necessary. **However**, government funding to pay for our research is limited. **Moreover**, few private companies are interested in funding this type of study. **Nevertheless**, my team will carry on with our research plans for as long as we can. This means that we may not be able to achieve all of our goals by the end of this year. **On the other hand**, we have already made some interesting discoveries, which I will now explain to you.

G Put the words from Exercise F in the correct category.

Agreeing with a point, or adding further information to support an idea or point:

1 _____
2 _____
3 _____

Disagreeing with a point, or offering an alternative idea or piece of information:

1 _____
2 _____
3 _____

Note: Some of the above phrases are almost identical in meaning. For example, 'moreover' and 'furthermore' mean the same thing. In this case, we might choose one instead of the other to avoid repetition, and to make a report more interesting.

H Now write a report on your findings from Exercise E. Use two of the taboos in the table from Exercise C. Follow the model below. Remember to use the vocabulary from Exercise F.

Title: Report on Cross-Cultural Taboos

Introduction (20–35 words)

Subtitle: (taboo 1)
Who I interviewed (30 words)
Results (30 words)

Subtitle: (taboo 2)
Who I interviewed (30 words)
Results (30 words)

Conclusion (20–35 words)

> ■ EXAMPLE
>
> *Who I interviewed:*
> *I interviewed two people from Mexico, one from France, one from Russia and one from Spain. However, I was unable to interview anyone from an Asian country.*
>
> *Result:*
> *Three people disagreed that (spitting in the street) was taboo in their country. On the other hand, there were two people who agreed that (spitting in the street) was taboo.*

Reading and Writing

A You are going to read about some of the rules of 'netiquette'. Before you read, discuss with a partner what you think 'netiquette' means.

B Now read this article about 'netiquette'. Then, complete the exercises that follow.

How to behave in Cyberspace

What does 'netiquette' mean? 'Netiquette' is a term that simply means Internet etiquette, or the rules of good online manners. Do you practise good 'netiquette'? If you don't, or aren't sure you do, then maybe now is the time to start.

Guideline 1 _____
Don't forget that you're not just communicating with a machine. There's a real person on the other end. It's easy to forget that when you're using a computer. That's why you should ask yourself if what you are writing is something you would say to that person's face. If the answer is 'no', you probably shouldn't send it.

Guideline 2 _____
We all receive emails we don't want from people trying to sell us something (spammers). The best thing to do is use your personal judgement. Use the same judgement as when someone offers you something you don't want in the 'real world'.

Guideline 3 _____
There are communities on the Internet, too. Especially when you join an online discussion group, take some time to read previous discussions and to learn what is considered appropriate in this particular community.

Guideline 4 _____
In this day and age, everybody is busy, and time is money. Make sure you don't waste other peoples' time online. When you use other people's bandwidth unwisely, you're bothering everyone. Ask yourself if it's really necessary to send so much information, or to attach such a large file with your message.

Guideline 5 _____
Remember that, online, the only 'image' a person has of you is your words. So grammar and spelling count! Moreover, you should know what you're talking about. Does what you're writing make sense? And is it polite? Be nice. Bad language or harsh criticism (known as flaming) isn't well mannered and can really upset people.

Guideline 6 _____
You may have seen some online discussion groups or forums where people like to flame each other. And yes, some people can really deserve it. But don't forget to check if it's an appropriate environment for this kind of communication.

Guideline 7 _____
This is probably good advice in real life, too. Be a good citizen. It's polite to show appreciation when people help us. Consider that someone took time from his or her schedule to help you. It's only fair that you thank them and maybe even pass the information on.

Guideline 8 _____
Do I really have to say that you shouldn't read other people's emails? This should be obvious. However, there will always be people who disrespect our privacy, so make sure you protect yourself by keeping your Internet passwords private.

Guideline 9 _____
There is always someone out there who knows more. These people, like magic, can do anything with a computer. And if you're one of them, don't misuse your power.

Guideline 10 _____
Remember, you were new to the Internet once. Have some patience with new users and be kind. Also, just because you have good manners, doesn't mean you have the right to tell others how to behave. Telling other people about things like spelling mistakes or how to act online is also considered bad netiquette!

C These are the correct titles for each guideline from Exercise B. Can you put them in the correct gap?

Respect others' time

Follow your usual values and beliefs

Forgive people's mistakes

Do some research before joining a discussion

Be careful not to abuse your power

Remember the human being

Make a good online impression

Do your part to keep flaming under control

Respect privacy

Thank and share

D Discuss the following questions.

1 How many of the 'netiquette' guidelines do you follow?

2 How many of the guidelines have you broken?

3 Are there any guidelines missing?

4 What really offends you when you are online or reading emails?

5 Have you ever offended anyone online? What happened?

6 Do you behave differently online than when you are talking to people face to face? How?

7 Which guideline do you think is most important? Why?

Look for examples of good and bad netiquette in these emails.

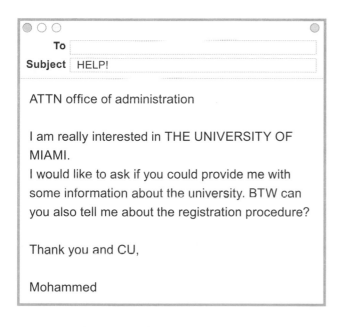

To
Subject HELP!

ATTN office of administration

I am really interested in THE UNIVERSITY OF MIAMI.
I would like to ask if you could provide me with some information about the university. BTW can you also tell me about the registration procedure?

Thank you and CU,

Mohammed

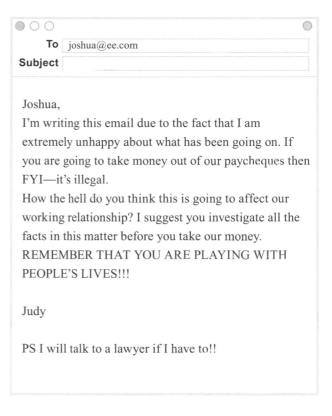

To joshua@ee.com
Subject

Joshua,
I'm writing this email due to the fact that I am extremely unhappy about what has been going on. If you are going to take money out of our paycheques then FYI—it's illegal.
How the hell do you think this is going to affect our working relationship? I suggest you investigate all the facts in this matter before you take our money.
REMEMBER THAT YOU ARE PLAYING WITH PEOPLE'S LIVES!!!

Judy

PS I will talk to a lawyer if I have to!!

To alicia
Subject surprise party

Hey Alicia,

FYI—surprise party for my best friend Shirley.
It's this Saturday. You have to dress to impress. There will be a guest singer there. And she will be the only one singing. YOU WILL NOT!!!!!!
The party is in a club in Manhattan. Everyone will be there, so don't miss it. OTOH, knowing you, you will. LOL

If you need more information, call me or email me back.

Regards,

Jennifer

F Here are some acronyms that are frequently used in emails. Match each acronym with its meaning.

1	ATTN	☐	☐ a	for your information
2	BTW	☐	☐ b	see you
3	CU	☐	☐ c	post script (meaning 'and another thing ... ')
4	IMO	☐		
5	FAQ	☐	☐ d	rolling on the floor laughing
6	FYI	☐	☐ e	on the other hand
7	OTOH	☐	☐ f	in my opinion
8	LOL	☐	☐ g	laughing out loud
9	ROTFL	☐	☐ h	attention
10	PS	☐	☐ i	by the way
			☐ j	frequently asked question/s

Homework

Write an email to your partner telling them about your time at EF. Use some of the acronyms and break some of the netiquette rules. Then send your email to your partner. Read the email your partner sent you and try to correct the mistakes you find.

Speaking

A You are going to plan and prepare a presentation on something that you have studied in this unit. Your presentation should contain each of the following elements:

- An icebreaker to start the presentation. This could be a short quiz, a role play or some questions. The aim of the icebreaker is to grab the attention of everyone in your group and involve them in your presentation.

- Some visual aids to make your presentation more interesting. These could include diagrams, graphs or photographs that illustrate your topic. Be imaginative.

- If you carried out some research on any topics in this unit, give your findings in your presentation. Collect statistics and think about how you will present the information to your group.

- A conclusion. Remember to draw all the information in your presentation together at the end. You can end the presentation with a statement of your opinion, or a question for your group to discuss.

Here are some suggestions for presentation topics. However, feel free to use your own ideas.

1   Tips on Good Behaviour in Your Country

Activity:
Role play a situation and the rest of the class must guess what you are doing wrong.

Presentation bullet points:
- Good manners
- Bad manners
- How to behave on the street and in a restaurant
- Language

2   Stereotypes

Use the information from the surveys you carried out in earlier lessons.
What stereotypes did people have about the country you live in / your country?
What conclusions can you make from the information you collected?
Turn the answers from your questionnaire into statistics. For example:
50% of the people I questioned thought that people in the UK are very polite.
Only 10% of the people I questioned thought that people in the UK are rude.

3   Netiquette

Activity:
Give a short quiz on acronyms. Do research and find some new ones that the class aren't familiar with.

Presentations:
Provide a clear summary of the rules and examples of their use or misuse.

Other ideas:
Add any personal email disaster stories. For example, have you ever sent an email to the wrong person?

4 Culture Shock

Activity:
Ask a student to tell the class about an experience they had when they first came to a new country that shocked them. Ask the class for advice.

Presentation:
Part 1—Using a visual graph on the whiteboard, explain the four stages of culture shock.
Part 2—Include a summary of the information in your surveys from earlier in the week.
Part 3—Talk about strategies you have used to deal with culture shock.

B Now plan your presentation. You should include timing, activity plans, information you wish to include and brief notes on what you are going to say. Remember, having too many notes in front of you will make your presentation less natural, so keep it simple! Use this page to help you organise your presentation, but don't read aloud from it when you give your presentation. (You may want to write some prompts on small pieces of paper so you don't forget what to say.)

Target length of presentation _____

Icebreaker activity:

Introduction:

Survey results:

Interesting statistics:

First point:

Second point:

Third point:

Conclusion:

Visual aids:

C Give your presentation and then ask your group for feedback. Complete the notes below.

What was good about my presentation? _____

What could I improve about my presentation? _____

Was the timing of my presentation good? _____

Did I involve the group in my presentation successfully? _____

Were my visual aids interesting and attractive? _____

How can I improve my next presentation? _____

Language Practice

A Match the adjectives in the first column with a phrase from the second column. Then use your match to write a complete sentence. (Note: there are more than seven correct answers.)

Some adjectives can be followed by infinitives.

┌─ ■ **EXAMPLES** ──────────────────
│ *Pleased to meet you.*
│ *It's polite to open the front door.*
└────────────────────────────────────

Often, these adjectives describe a person's feelings or attitudes.

┌─ ■ **EXAMPLES** ──────────────────
│ *I was excited to buy tickets.*
│ *I was afraid to say anything.*
└────────────────────────────────────

1	sad	☐	☐	a	to do
2	happy	☐	☐	b	to help
3	lucky	☐	☐	c	to be
4	prepared	☐	☐	d	to see
5	good	☐	☐	e	to know
6	eager	☐	☐	f	to have
7	nice	☐	☐	g	to hear

1 _____
_____
2 _____
_____
3 _____
_____
4 _____
_____
5 _____
_____
6 _____
_____
7 _____
_____

B Write sentences with the words below.

1 careful _____
2 ashamed _____
3 ready _____
4 surprised _____
5 proud _____

C Use the words below to make sentences.

1 Michael / lucky / be / alive after the accident
_____

2 Mrs Alston / always / ready / help us / when / we young
_____

3 The twins / eager / go / the circus / next Sunday
_____

4 Jim / hesitant / play / American football / when / student
_____

5 I / sorry / hear / about your sick brother
_____

6 Anders / proud / win / Olympic swimming medal
_____

7 Toby / scared / try / acupuncture
_____

8 My father / ready / retire / in two years
_____

D Choose an infinitive to fill each gap.

1 Christian is afraid _____ his mother that he failed his exam.
2 It's impolite _____ with your mouth full!
3 It's polite _____ in your chair when you leave the dinner table.
4 Were you happy _____ that you passed your test?
5 Mauricia is getting bored with her job. In fact, she is ready _____.
6 Victor had such a good time he was sad _____.
7 Hey! It's good _____ you! It's been a long time!
8 I was sorry _____ about your exam result.
9 It was nice _____ my brother on the phone last night.
10 I was surprised _____ John yesterday. I thought he was ill.

E Write a paragraph on the topic below, using all the words and phrases in the box. Look back at the text on page 105, Exercise F, if you need help with style.

The legal age for drinking alcohol in the USA should be 18, not 21. After all, at 18, people are considered to be adults.

1 furthermore	2 in addition
3 on the other hand	4 however
5 moreover	6 nevertheless

F Now fill the gaps with the vocabulary from Exercise E. More than one answer will be possible in each case. Try to use each word / phrase you learnt.

When you visit the United States, it's a good idea to remember your manners. Americans like people to be polite. _____, they will probably help you more if you are polite to them. _____, you should also try to relax and have fun. Americans are friendly and sociable. They like to meet people from different cultures.

_____, don't expect every encounter to be a polite one. Just like everywhere else in the world, there will always be people who are rude. _____, the level of politeness will be different from place to place.

Another thing you shouldn't do is judge the people too quickly. Many people have a preset idea about Americans and their culture. _____, most Americans probably have stereotypes for your country and culture as well. It's important not to forget the way you feel when someone judges you without knowing you. You may be tempted to react like you would in your own country. _____, you must consider that you are a guest in the USA and need to be patient. This way, you will be able to enjoy your visit more!

G Fill the gaps with the infinitive of these words.

watch   eat   go   hear   survive   open   play
run   say   see   sleep   stay   lose   work   invite

1   She was lucky _____ the earthquake.
2   I was hoping _____ the movie.
3   It is polite _____ 'thank you'.
4   I am afraid _____ home alone.
5   Were you surprised _____ me?
6   Terry was sorry _____ the bad news.
7   I'm proud _____ goalkeeper on my football team.
8   Roy is hesitant _____ in the marathon.
9   I was disappointed _____ the contest.
10 It's polite _____ the door for someone.

H Now try to write sentences about yourself using this structure. Use the remaining verbs from Exercise G and adjectives of your own.

I Discuss what you think would be good manners in the following situations. What would be a polite thing to do in each situation? What would it be impolite to do?

1   when you are eating dinner
2   when you meet someone for the first time
3   when someone sneezes
4   when you leave the dinner table
5   when you ask for something
6   when someone gives you a present

J Now write some sentences giving advice on how to behave in each of the above situations. Think of the words and phrases you have learnt in this unit.

Language Reference

ADJECTIVES + INFINITIVES

Many common adjectives can be followed by an infinitive. Examples include: right, wrong, stupid, certain, welcome, careful, due, fit, able, likely and lucky.

You were right to sell your house when you did.

Shergar was certain to win the race.

Please be careful not to get mud on the chairs.

I hope Rooney will be judged fit to play in the World Cup.

Driving at that speed, he'll be lucky not to crash his car.

We sometimes use infinitives after adjectives to describe people's reactions and feelings.

I was upset to hear you got divorced.

She was very surprised to win the prize.

Peter was happy to be invited to the concert by Melissa.

(BE) USED TO

'(Be) used to' is often used to describe a situation when someone is very familiar with or comfortable with something.

I was so used to seeing Tom every day that I missed him a lot when he went away.

Are you used to British food yet?

I wasn't used to driving on the right side of the road.

'(Be) used to' can be followed by a noun or a gerund, but not by an infinitive. 'Used' is an adjective in this structure.

Mohammed wasn't used to washing his own clothes.

I'm so used to Russian winters that I don't mind them anymore.

moving forward

After this unit, you should be able to ...

- Implement reading strategies to improve your reading skills
- Present a mini grammar lesson to your classmates
- Analyse, identify and write in different text types
- Compare customs around the world
- Understand defining and non-defining relative clauses

A How fast do you read? Do you think you could improve your reading speed? Work with a partner. Using a watch or the classroom clock, take turns doing the following activities.

1 Read the following paragraph twice. Record the seconds or minutes it takes you to do this.

First time _____

Second time _____

Western *visitors* to China *quickly* notice that the rules of **etiquette** they bring with them do not always apply to the Chinese **context**. Etiquette is *based* on social values, and *in order* to understand Chinese etiquette, visitors need an **understanding** of one particularly **fundamental** Chinese *social* value, the *value* that *anthropologists* refer to as '**collectivism**'.

The easiest way to understand collectivism is to contrast it with individualism, a fundamental **value** in most *societies* of Europe, **North** America, Australia and New Zealand. Societies based on individualism make individual rights the starting **point** for their value **system**. Societies based on **collectivism**, on the *other* hand, see the **collective**, or the social group, as the **starting** point for *their* value **system**.

2 Do you remember what you read? Write down some things you remember (words, phrases or complete ideas).

3 How many words were there that you didn't understand? Tick the box.

one or two ☐   a few ☐   many ☐

B Work with a partner. Some of the words in the previous paragraph are in **boldface**.

Your partner will count to ten slowly. Try to read out loud as many boldfaced words as you can in the ten seconds. Your partner will circle the words you read in his or her book.

Now it's your partner's turn. Your partner will read the words that are in *italics*. You will count to ten slowly and circle the words he or she reads out loud.

1 How many words did you read in ten seconds?
2 How many boldfaced words are there in total?
3 How many words did your partner read?
4 How many italicized words ara there in total?

Reading

A Discuss the following questions.

1 Do you enjoy reading in your native language? How about reading in English?

2 How fast can you read in English?

3 How often do you read? What do you like to read?

4 How important is it to you to develop your reading skills in English? Why?

5 How does your skill in reading compare to your other English skills (speaking, for example)?

6 Can reading help you with other language skills, such as speaking and listening? How?

7 When you read a text in English, do you use any special strategies to help you?

8 When you come to an unfamiliar word in a text, do you usually look it up in the dictionary immediately? Why or why not?

9 Has your reading improved since you started learning English? Why or why not?

10 What do you find most difficult about reading in English?

B Here are four strategies from a book on study skills. Match a heading to each strategy.

Study skills	• Read quickly	• Read what interests you
	• Limit your dictionary use	• Start with the topic

Strategy Number 1 _____

When you read in a foreign language, the first thing you need to do is put your dictionary in an inconvenient place. Now you are probably thinking, 'Doesn't she mean a convenient place?' And the answer to that is, 'No, I don't. I mean an inconvenient place.' The biggest mistake most people make when they are learning to read in another language is that they depend too much on their dictionary. Try to read for general meaning, and don't worry about the words you don't know. If you come across a new word, try to keep reading; often you can guess the meaning of the word from the context. Take a look, for example, at the following two sentences:

The movie was ijjish. I laughed really hard.

Did you want to get your dictionary when you saw the word 'ijjish'? If you looked 'ijjish' up in the dictionary, you would be disappointed, because you cannot find 'ijjish' in any dictionary. If, however, you continued reading, the next sentence made the meaning clear for you.

Strategy Number 2 _____

Many people are surprised by this strange strategy. They think that slow, careful reading must lead to better comprehension than fast reading. In fact, when you read quickly, you are reading several words at the same time, and your brain can process the meaning of the words more efficiently. When you read one or two words at a time, your brain has to work much harder, because it needs to process each word separately and relate each word to the words that came before.

Try reading this sentence:
You should stay
away from buildings
during an earthquake.

Now try reading this sentence:
During an earthquake, you should get under a table.

Which sentence was faster and easier to read? Most people would say that the second sentence was easier. The layout of the first sentence forces you to read more slowly and read each word individually, and that is a much less effective way to read.

Strategy Number 3 _____

You will find it much easier to understand a text if you know what the topic or main idea is before you begin reading. Knowing the topic—and thinking about it—helps you predict the content of the text. For example, if you know that a newspaper article is going to be about an earthquake, you will probably expect it to include information about damage to buildings. Your expectations will help you guess word meaning in context.

But how can you know the topic before you start reading? Often the title will give you a clue. Or there might be pictures accompanying the text. And, of course, the first few sentences usually point the way.

After you have identified the topic or main idea, it is a good idea to talk about it with other people. This will make you think about the topic in different ways. The more ways you think about the topic, the easier it will be to make predictions about the content. Talking can also stimulate your interest in the topic, which will increase your desire to read about it.

Strategy Number 4 _____

The best readers are those who read often. As with any other skill, practice makes perfect. When you have a choice, choose texts that are truly interesting to you. The more a text interests you, the more it will help you develop your reading skills and, of course, it is a lot more fun to read something that interests you than to read something that bores you!

C Read the text again and answer the questions.

1 What does the author say you should do with your dictionary when you read?

_____

2 Why is it better to read quickly?

_____

3 What do you think the imaginary word 'ijjish' means? How do you know?

_____

4 Why is it helpful to talk about the topic of a text before you read the text?

_____

5 What kind of texts does the author recommend?

_____

D Strategy Number 2 talks about how reading faster can help you read more efficiently. How many words do you read at a time? Fast readers usually read several words at a time. However, it's important to know just which words you should read together.

Put a ' ✓ ' before the groups of words that are easy to read together and an ' X ' before those that aren't.

- _____ try to read
- _____ but how can
- _____ when you
- _____ the best readers are
- _____ No, I don't
- _____ This will make you
- _____ The movie was
- _____ I laughed really
- _____ the more ways you think
- _____ when you come to an unfamiliar word

Grammar

A Look at the following list of grammar points. Can you think of an example sentence for each point?

1 future with 'going to' _____
2 future with 'will' _____
3 gerund _____
4 past continuous _____
5 simple past _____
6 'used to' _____
7 adjective + infinitive _____
8 second conditional _____
9 zero conditional _____

B The following dialogue contains examples of the above grammar points. Read the dialogue.

Elizabeth: I'm so glad I read the article on how to improve my reading skills. Now, I realise reading can really help me with my English progress.

Paul: How so?

Elizabeth: I was doing everything wrong when I was reading. For example, I used to look up lots of words in my dictionary. This made reading really boring and time consuming. I remember that one time I was looking up one word and got distracted by another word from the dictionary. This happened a lot, actually.

Paul: I do that all the time! And you say I shouldn't?

Elizabeth: No! You have to try and read for meaning and not worry about every word. And reading slowly is also a mistake. If you read slowly—like one or two words at a time—your brain works much harder.

Paul: No wonder I'm no good at reading. So what should I do to improve?

Elizabeth: If I were you, I'd practise reading three or four words at a time until you can read a whole sentence. It's so much easier this way.

Paul: I see the logic in that. I'm going to try to read faster by reading more words at a time. I'll try it with my next homework assignment.

Elizabeth: Believe me, it's so nice to read when you do it the right way.

Paul: Thanks Liz, I'm going to try to do what you suggest. I'll let you know what happens, OK?

Elizabeth: Sure. See you around.

C Complete the table with examples from the dialogue.

Grammar point	Examples from dialogue
future with 'going to'	I'm going to try to do what you suggest.
future with 'will'	
gerund	
past continuous	
simple past	
'used to'	
adjective + infinitive	
second conditional	
zero conditional	

D Work with a partner. Answer the questions about some of the grammar points. You can look back at the dialogue to check your answers.

Future with 'going to'
Does this express a plan? _____
Is this plan 100% sure? _____

Future with 'will'
Does this express an intention? _____
Is it something you decide to do suddenly, or something you decide to do far in advance?

_____

'used to'
Is this used to talk about something you do now?

_____

Is this about something you did frequently in your past? _____

E Choose one of the grammar points from Exercise A. How would you teach this grammar point to a new learner of English? Prepare a short lesson. Include structure, use and meaning. Include three questions for the class to answer.

1 What is this grammar point used for?

_____

2 What is the structure of this grammar point? (Think about the type of words / tense it uses.)

_____

3 Give some examples of this grammar point to illustrate what it is used for.

_____

4 What is difficult to understand about this grammar point?

_____

5 Think of three questions your students must answer about this grammar point.

_____
_____
_____

F Present your lesson to the class. Grade your lesson: If students answer all three questions correctly, give yourself an 'A'. If they answer two questions correctly, give yourself a 'B'. If they answer only one question correctly, give yourself a 'C'. If students can tell you when to use this grammar point, give yourself a star.

G Answer the questions about the dialogue in Exercise B. Use the correct grammar structures in your answers.

1 What does Paul plan to do to improve his reading skills? _____
2 What did Elizabeth do before that she doesn't do now? _____
3 What does Elizabeth think now about reading?

_____

4 When will Paul use the new ideas about reading? _____

H Fill the gaps in the following sentences. Next to the sentence, write the matching letter from the grammar point list in Exercise A.

┌─── ■ EXAMPLE ───────────────────┐
│ *John and I are* _____ *have dinner with some* │
│ *friends tomorrow.* ____ │
└───────────────────────────────────┘

1 While I _____ along the road, a bus almost hit me! _____
2 When I was a child, we _____ have a dog called Petu. _____
3 I like _____, but I haven't got a bike! _____
4 If computers were cheaper, I _____ buy a new one. _____
5 Ice _____ if it gets hot. _____
6 I was sorry _____ about your mother's illness. _____
7 Where are your keys? I _____ help you look for them, OK? _____
8 Are you _____ visit your friends tomorrow? _____
9 On the way home, I _____ to the shop to buy a newspaper. _____

Reading and Speaking

A Can you remember the four reading strategies from pages 114-115? Try to answer without looking back.

B How much do you know about Latin America?

1 Name four countries in Latin America. _____

2 Is more than one language spoken in Latin American countries? _____

3 Where exactly is Latin America? _____

C Read the following text. Read it quickly and decide which title is the best.

Latin America and its people	Latin America offers more than just beaches
Latin America is full of traditions	Latin Americans are very different to people from other cultures

When people think of Latin America, they immediately imagine beautiful beaches, tropical weather, spicy food and, of course, the very rhythmic music and dances. But what about its culture? Latin America is a place full of traditions, folklore and customs which influence family, work, and even the way people behave in the streets. It is a place of 'chivalry'.

The heart of every Latin American family is the mother. All events, holidays and decisions surround her. The most important areas of a house are the dining room and the back yard. Here is where families partake in the most important activities: eating, dancing, drinking and spending hour after hour talking. The women talk about the latest gossip and entertainment news or about what's going on with their neighbours. The men usually talk about sports or get into heated arguments about politics.

There are so many rules of etiquette that there is a book that children are expected to study in school to help them learn how to behave. For example, if you are invited for dinner in a Latin American house, make sure you take something to drink or eat to offer the family. It can be some fruit, a dessert or a bottle of wine. While you eat, you will feel like a king or queen because all the attention will be bestowed on you. You get to try the wine first, to eat the first piece of cake and even be the one to say grace (a short prayer of thanksgiving said before a meal).

When Latin Americans expect a guest to stay for a week or more, they make sure that there is a bouquet of flowers waiting in the room where they will sleep. And, of course, the guest gets the best room or 'alcoba' of the house, even if this means everyone else sleeps in discomfort.

When you meet someone for the first time, the 'hello' is accompanied by a kiss on the cheek and followed by a soft warm hug. And the kissing rituals don't stop here. You kiss the person when you come in, and then again when you leave. If there are ten people in the room ... guess what? You have to kiss everybody or they will be offended. Dating is one more event full of important traditions. When a Latin American girl goes on a first date, the man has to pick her up at her house so he can meet her family. After the date, he must make sure he accompanies her home, no matter how far away he may live. The couple may also have to go on their first date with a 'chaperone' if the girl's family is very traditional.

In the business world, meetings begin in an office and then finish at a restaurant. Also, at work, if someone has a university degree or is a boss, they are addressed as 'Doctor'. It is considered important to address people correctly.

Riding a bus can be fun. First of all, the buses are very picturesque on the outside and inside. They might even have elaborate curtains on their windows. There is usually loud music playing all the time and people come on board throughout the ride just to sell things that can range from candy to CDs and even household items. Oh, and if you have lots of bags or even just a couple of heavy books and there are no seats available, someone who is sitting down will offer to carry these things for you on their lap. Be warned, saying 'no' to such cordial gestures is considered very offensive.

Latin America is famous for its breathtaking landscapes. But the people should also be remembered, for they are very hospitable, amicable and family-oriented and have many interesting and important traditions and customs.

D Read the text again. Underline any words you don't understand. Try to write a definition for each based on the context.

E Work with a partner and use a dictionary to check the definitions.

F Read the text again quickly. Find the following information.

1 What should you expect to happen on a bus in Latin America?
2 When is the title of 'Doctor' used?
3 Explain what happens on a first date.
4 What is a 'chaperone'?
5 Who is the heart of every Latin American family?
6 What are Latin Americans like?
7 If you are a guest for dinner, what do you need to bring with you?
8 Describe how you picture the curtains in the buses based on what you read.
9 What things will offend Latin Americans?
10 Which of these traditions, customs or rules of etiquette did you find most different from those of your country?

G Now work with a partner. Take turns answering the questions from Exercise F fully. Try to use your own words, rather than reading straight from the text.

H Part of being a successful reader involves following instructions carefully. Using the text on page 118, follow the instructions below.

1 Circle the words that are in quotation marks.
2 Underline the verbs in lines 1 through 16.
3 Complete the following sentences that use 'when'.
When Latin Americans _____
_____
_____

When you meet _____
_____

4 Put a box around what happens if you are invited for dinner.
5 Find the word that means 'someone who accompanies you on a date'.
_____

6 Write synonyms for the following words in the text: breathtaking, picturesque, cordial, elaborate.
_____

I Interview a classmate. Ask him / her questions about the customs in his / her country associated with the situations below. Are things done differently in your country? (If your partner comes from the same country as you, compare your traditions with those of another country you have both studied.)

bus rides
having a guest stay over
at the dinner table
greeting people
the heart of the family
doing business
dating

Listening and Speaking

 A At what age do people usually start working? Have you ever had a part-time job? Listen to four teenagers talk about working.

 B Listen again. Are the statements below True or False?

1 **T F** JP thinks working at Super Burger is a good idea.
2 **T F** Mariela is going to work for a designer when she starts her first job.
3 **T F** JP thinks that people who work at Super Burger soon leave their job.
4 **T F** Sonia's father used to wait on tables before he bought his own restaurant.
5 **T F** Mark thinks working at Super Burger is not a bad idea.
6 **T F** Sonia is not going to wait until she is 18 to start working.
7 **T F** Mark is going to start his own business.
8 **T F** Sonia thinks she should start working now because her father started at 15.
9 **T F** Sonia and Mariela have never worked before.
10 **T F** Mariela probably has more money than Sonia.

C In groups of three, discuss the following questions.

1 What is the best age to start working?
2 Are there any specific laws in your country regarding working at an early age?
3 Name some typical 'first jobs'.
4 Have you ever worked? How old were you when you started? What did you do? How much did you earn?
5 What are the advantages and disadvantages of starting to work very young?

D In your groups, think about Sonia's father's success.

1 How do you think he got to be owner of his own restaurant?
2 What jobs did he probably do before actually becoming a restaurant owner?
3 Did his age at the beginning influence his success? How?
4 Do you know anyone who was successful before the age of 21?

Homework

Use newspapers, magazines and the Internet to research one of the following topics. Gather information about your topic and prepare a short presentation. Then try to include the points on the right in your presentation.

Topics

- Business icons who achieved success young (e.g., Richard Branson of Virgin Airlines and Martha Lane Fox of Lastminute.com)
- Child labour in the third world (countries where many children have to work include Bangladesh and Tanzania)
- How to balance work and study
- Entrepreneurship (why young people should make their own business opportunities)

1 A brief introduction to the topic (Why did you choose it? Why is it interesting?)
2 Some facts and statistics about your topic (for example, Richard Branson had made his first million by the time he was ...)
3 What we can learn from these facts and statistics?
4 A brief conclusion

Listening and Pronunciation

A Listen to the questions and write them in the space provided. Then, choose the best answer to each question.

1 _____

 a They like them.
 b They're old.
 c No, it wasn't.
 d It's modern.

2 _____

 a They're beautiful.
 b They look in the mirror.
 c They don't like it.
 d Yes, they do.

3 _____

 a It doesn't feel like it.
 b I feel like going to the movies.
 c It's smooth.
 d No, it doesn't.

4 _____

 a He likes Amy.
 b He doesn't feel like it.
 c No, he doesn't.
 d He's like his father.

5 _____

 a Yes, I am.
 b Yes, I do.
 c My brother.
 d It doesn't agree with me.

6 _____

 a She's wrong.
 b She has a bad headache.
 c Yes, she was.
 d She's with Fred.

7 _____

 a It was too expensive.
 b They didn't buy it.
 c They buy it.
 d No, they didn't.

8 _____

 a You sing.
 b I'm an acupuncturist.
 c I'm singing.
 d I went skiing.

B Can you remember the rules for the pronunciation of the final '-ed' of regular simple past verbs? What are the three possible sounds for '-ed'? Write them in the boxes below, then, underneath each sound, write some examples.

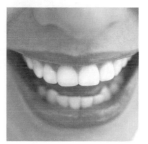

[   ]   [   ]   [   ]
_____   _____   _____

Listening and Pronunciation

C Look at the following words. How is the '-ed' pronounced? Write the answer in the space provided.

> **■ EXAMPLE**
>
> *parked*   / t /

1 shouted   _____
2 called   _____
3 yelled   _____
4 played   _____
5 walked   _____
6 nodded   _____
7 showed   _____
8 loaded   _____
9 knocked   _____
10 started   _____

D Now listen to the words. Were you correct?

E Read the following sentences. Underline the stressed words in each sentence and decide how the final '-ed' in the verbs should be pronounced.

1 As I <u>passed</u> the <u>man</u> in the <u>street</u>, he <u>kicked</u> me <u>hard</u> in the <u>leg</u>.
2 I <u>turned</u> around and <u>shouted</u> at him. Then he <u>pushed</u> me and <u>laughed</u>!
3 I <u>punched</u> him in the <u>stomach</u>, but he was <u>wearing</u> a <u>padded</u> <u>jacket</u>, so he <u>didn't</u> <u>feel</u> <u>anything</u>.
4 A <u>passing</u> <u>policeman</u> <u>stopped</u> and <u>told</u> us we would be in <u>big</u> <u>trouble</u> if we <u>didn't</u> <u>stop</u> <u>fighting</u>.
5 The man <u>apologised</u> and we <u>shook</u> <u>hands</u>.

F Now practise saying each sentence to your partner. Try not to overstress any words. Speak fast and naturally!

G Look at the words below. Say each word out loud, then circle the correct symbol for the vowel sound in each word.

> **■ EXAMPLES**
>
> *cat*   (/ æ /)   / e /

1 black	/ æ /	/ eɪ /
2 shed	/ aɪ /	/ e /
3 block	/ ɒ /	/ ʌ /
4 pick	/ ɪ /	/ i: /
5 a	/ ə /	/ ʌ /
6 foot	/ ʌ /	/ ʊ /
7 cup	/ ʌ /	/ ʊ /
8 we	/ i: /	/ æ /
9 far	/ ɑ: /	/ ɜ: /
10 shoe	/ u: /	/ ɒ /
11 fur	/ ɜ: /	/ ɑ: /
12 play	/ æ /	/ eɪ /
13 five	/ aɪ /	/ i: /
14 now	/ ʌ /	/ aʊ /
15 toy	/ ɔɪ /	/ aɪ /
16 near	/ ɪə /	/ i: /
17 rare	/ ɜ: /	/ eə /

H Now listen to the words. Were you correct?

Homework

Choose the two sounds from Exercise G that you have most difficulty pronouncing correctly. Write a list of words that contain the sounds, then, write a few sentences containing some of the words. Write them phonetically, if possible. At home, practise pronouncing the sounds, the words and the sentences. Note the shape your mouth makes when pronouncing the sounds correctly. Practise each day until your next class.

Writing

A We have read different text types in the units in this level. Look at the following examples. Try to match the type of text with the correct description.

  a magazine article
  b newspaper article
  c email
  d recipe
  e letter

_____ This type of text is written by a journalist, but it isn't always news. Popular articles of this type deal with 'human interest' stories like interviews with celebrities, stories about real-life people or in-depth information about products like cars or makeup.

_____ These days, pretty much everyone writes text of this type. We use computers to send this type of text to our business colleagues, friends and family. We can attach documents and pictures to these texts. Some of us send and receive hundreds of these every day.

_____ In recent years, this type of text has become less common, although it is still very important. Businesspeople send and receive this type of text when electronic texts are not suitable. This type of text is printed on paper. It may be typed or handwritten, and can vary from a wedding invitation to an important legal document.

_____ This type of text can be seen in newsagents every day. It is usually printed in black and white, and is used to tell us important news. This news can be local, national or international. Journalists write this type of text. This type of text is normally thrown away the day after it is printed.

_____ When we want to cook something special, we read this type of text. It usually consists of simple instructions, printed in a book and accompanied by colourful pictures of ingredients and dishes. Text of this type is most often kept in the kitchen.

B Read these sentences and match them to the appropriate text type (a–e). There may be more than one correct answer for some sentences.

1 First of all, take an onion and chop it finely. _____
2 A man dressed in a Santa Claus suit was seen running from the bank. _____
3 How's it going? I'm having a great time:-) RU coming to the party later? _____
4 Further to your correspondence of 25 March, I am writing to confirm ... _____
5 So what really makes us tick? John Marr thinks he knows. _____
6 Do not let the milk boil. _____
7 John Smith was convicted and sentenced to two life terms. _____
8 I am writing to ask for more information about the job. _____
9 Our experts test-drive the new Porsche! _____
10 The incident occurred early this morning near the post office on 23rd St. _____
11 You have just received an e-card from Cathy. _____
12 Yours sincerely, Mr Johnson _____
13 Cut the tomatoes into thin slices. _____
14 The real-life scandal of the man with 49 children! _____

Writing

C Look at the samples on the right and make some notes about the form of each text.

> ### ■ EXAMPLE
> *Magazine article:*
> * *Stories about real people*
> * *In-depth interviews*
> * *Bright, glossy photographs accompany article*

Newspaper article:

> **INSIDE**
> **Regus calls off merger talks**
> **Hays slides after prof...**
> PROBLEMS IN LOGISTICS DIVISION AT BUSINESS SERVICES GROUP...

Email:

> **To** mike guerrero
> **Subject** Re: Hi
>
> Hi
> It's great to know that you're coming, please let me know when you're going to arrive and where you are going to stay. My phone number is 56457743.
> Take care.
> Erika:-)

Recipe:

> **Lemonade** • *6 cups water* • *3/4 cup sugar* • *4 medium lemons*
>
>
> Place water and sugar in a jug. Mix well until sugar is dissolved. Zest lemons for 1 tablespoon of zest. Juice lemons for 1/2 cup of juice. Add juice and zest to jug. Mix well. Serve over ice and garnish with fresh mint and a slice of lemon.

Letter:

> Dear John,
>
> I am writing to inform you that your books are ready. Would you like us to send them to your home address?
>
> Sincerely,
> Mrs Belinda Smith
> Books Inc.

D Choose one of the forms and use your notes to help you write a text of a similar style. Think about the following questions before you begin to write.

1 How long should your text be?
2 What information must you include?
3 What tense should you write in?
4 Should the language be formal or informal? Should it be friendly or direct?
5 Will you need to include images or other attachments?

Grammar

A Complete the table below and write example questions of your own.

Question words	Uses	Examples
who	*people*	*Who is she?*
whose		
what		
what + like		
which		
where		
when		
why		
how		
how many		
how much		
how often		

B Sentences are made of one or more clauses. A common type of clause is the relative clause. Look at the examples below, and then answer the questions which follow.

> ■ EXAMPLES
>
> *Traffic wardens are the people who check to see if your car is parked in the right place.*
> *I'll ask Clare to marry me when the time is right.*
> *Michael Jackson's 'Thriller' is the album that has sold most copies worldwide.*

1 In the examples above, which words are used to introduce relative clauses?
_____

2 From reading the above examples, what would you say relative clauses are used for?
_____

3 In the third example, what other word could replace 'that'? _____

4 Write some example sentences containing relative clauses and the following words.
whose _____
where _____
which _____

C There are two types of relative clauses. Look at the examples below, and then answer the questions which follow.

> ■ EXAMPLES
>
> *The hospital where I was born is in Hendon.*
> *The hospital, where I was born, is in Hendon.*

1 What is the difference between the first and second example? _____
_____

2 What can you see in the second example that you can't see in the first? _____

3 What would happen to the meaning of the first sentence if the relative clause were removed?
_____

4 What would happen to the meaning of the second sentence if 'where I was born' were removed? _____

The first sentence is an example of a defining relative clause. In this type of sentence, the relative clause identifies or classifies the noun in the sentence (in this case, 'hospital').
The second sentence is an example of a non-defining relative clause. In this type of sentence, the relative clause does not identify or classify the noun, it simply adds more information. Non-defining relative clauses can generally be removed from a sentence without making it ungrammatical.

D Look at these examples and decide if the relative clause is defining or non-defining.

1 Pierre, who had studied Japanese for many years, could only speak French. _____

2 The houses, which have swimming pools, cost $300,000. _____

3 Temples are places where people go to pray or meditate. _____

4 Last year I sold my business, which went for $50,000. _____

5 People who talk loudly on buses really irritate me. _____

6 Is that your idea that I heard the boss talking about? _____

Language Practice

A   The exercises on these pages contain vocabulary and grammar from earlier units, too. Complete each sentence with a word from the box.

confidential	damaged	expert	lucky	manners
mature	outgoing	recommended	unemployed	retired

1   My parents _____ last year. They quit their jobs and moved to Mexico.

2   Toby is very _____. It is easy for him to make new friends.

3   You're _____ to have such a good job.

4   Is Margaret only 18? She's so _____! I thought she was much older.

5   Matt has been _____ for the past two years. He just can't find a job.

6   Kristina didn't know what to order. The waiter _____ the beef, so she got that.

7   Their house was badly _____ in the earthquake.

8   I can't tell you what Martha told me. It was _____.

9   Frances has terrible _____. Her mouth is always open when she's eating!

10   Her mother is an _____ on earthquakes. She knows everything about them.

B   Complete each sentence with one of the words or phrases in brackets.

> **■ EXAMPLE**
>
> *I'd like <u>to reserve</u> a room. (reserving / to reserve)*

1   What _____ she look like? (does / is)

2   What _____ the weather like? (does / is)

3   I'm going to travel when _____ get older. (I / I'll)

4   I'll talk with you while you _____ dinner. (are making / will make)

5   Before _____ to the movies, we should wash the dishes. (go / going)

6   My daughter wants to be a doctor when she grows _____. (out / up)

7   Did you _____ out what time the movie starts? (figure / find)

8   You _____ to get a job! (ought / should)

9   I was afraid _____ say anything. (of / to)

C   Match each sentence with an appropriate response. Use each response once.

1   We'll order 500 if you give us a discount. ☐   ☐ a It's light and fast.

2   Could I have a drink? ☐   ☐ b It's quite sweet.

3   Is age important to you? ☐   ☐ c It's loud.

4   What's your new bicycle like? ☐   ☐ d I totally disagree.

5   How old is it? ☐   ☐ e It's a deal.

6   What does it sound like? ☐   ☐ f That's not enough time.

7   I used to like it. ☐   ☐ g What would you like?

8   We need them by Friday. ☐   ☐ h So did I.

9   Trains are better than planes. ☐   ☐ i I don't know.

10   What does it taste like? ☐   ☐ j Yes, it is.

D Each of these sentences contains a mistake. Find the mistake, and then write the sentence correctly.

1 There are much more skyscrapers in New York than in Brussels.

_____

2 What does your new house looks like?

_____

3 They both look like friendly.

_____

4 It will probably snow tomorrow if it'll be as cold as this.

_____

5 I went for a walk as soon as I finish lunch.

_____

6 As soon as I receive your proposal, I'll make my best to respond to it.

_____

7 The doctors don't know what's wrong in me.

_____

8 Smoke cigarettes isn't good for your health.

_____

9 What should we do while an earthquake?

_____

10 Miranda use to go out with her friends every Friday night.

_____

E Work with a partner. Take turns doing each of the following exercises.

1 Look back at the text for Strategy Number 3 on page 115. Find the first sentence. Put a box around each word separately. Try to read the sentence to your partner.

2 In the third sentence, put a box around words or phrases that you think should be read together. Read the sentence to your partner.

3 Read the third paragraph (begins with 'After you…') out loud to your partner, only pausing when you see a comma (,) and only stopping at a full stop / period (.).

F In which of the following can you read several words at a time?

1 a newspaper article ☐
2 a recipe ☐
3 the subtitles to a movie ☐
4 a menu at a restaurant or fast food place ☐
5 instructions ☐
6 signs on the road ☐
7 lyrics to a song ☐
8 a card from a friend ☐
9 a letter ☐
10 an email ☐

G Correct the sentences.

1 While he played the piano, they were all listen quietly.

_____

2 If you had a horse, I will borrow it.

_____

3 I am very sad see you go.

_____

4 I will meet my friends at 6pm next Thursday.

_____

5 I am used to go to bed at 6 o'clock when I was young.

_____

6 Ride a bicycle is easy once you know how.

_____

7 I think I go out for dinner tonight.

_____

8 I'm very bad maths. It's my worst subject.

_____

Language Reference

QUESTION FORMS

There are two main types of question: 'Yes / No' questions and questions which begin with a question word such as 'What' or 'How' (so-called 'Wh-' questions).

'Yes / No' questions begin with the verb 'to be' or an auxiliary verb such as 'do' or 'have'. Try to answer these questions in a full sentence, not just with 'Yes' or 'No'.

Are you John? Yes, I am.

Do you drink coffee? No, I don't.

Have you been to Venice? Yes, I have.

'Wh-' questions begin with a question word and then the verb 'to be' or an auxiliary verb such as 'do' or 'have'. Depending on how much information is required, and how formal the conversation is, you can give long or short answers to these questions. If you are talking to a close friend and the conversation is quite informal, it's fine to use short answers. For more formal conversations, try to give your answer in a full sentence.

What is her name? Carole / Her name is Carole.

What are those buildings? Government offices / Those are government offices.

How did you do in your exams? OK / I did OK.

How many people are coming? 23 / 23 people are coming.

Why have you come here? To see John. / I'm here to see John.

Question words	Uses	Examples
who	people	*Who is the man over there?*
whose	possession	*Whose are those gloves?*
what	things	*What is this?*
what + like	descriptions	*What is your sister like?*
what + time	time	*What time does the concert start?*
which	clarification or decision	*Which do you prefer, the blue or the red?*
where	places	*Where does your father live?*
when	time and dates	*When is your birthday?*
why	reasons	*Why did you steal my hat?*
how	method	*How do you get to the airport?*
how many	numbers	*How many days are there in June?*
how much	quantity and price	*How much milk do we need?*
how old	age	*How old are your parents?*
how often	frequency	*How often do you see your brother?*

RELATIVE CLAUSES

There are two main types of relative clauses: defining and non-defining (sometimes called 'identifying' and 'non-identifying'). A defining relative clause is essential to the meaning of a sentence. A non-defining relative clause gives non-essential information about the subject.

Defining:

The man who bought my car was very tall.

Non-defining:

John, who bought my car, is very tall.

Relative clauses can be introduced with several different words: 'who', 'whom', 'that', 'which', 'whose', 'where', 'when' and 'why'.

Commas in relative clauses:

Defining clauses are usually written without commas.

Non-defining clauses are written with commas.

Defining:

The houses which have swimming pools cost $300,000.

(Only the houses which have swimming pools cost $300,000; those without swimming pools are a different price.)

Non-defining:

The houses, which have swimming pools, cost $300,000.

(All the houses have swimming pools, and they all cost $300,000.)

Appendix

iLab links

Unit 1 The spice of life

If you want to dine out, there are so many great places to choose from, it can often be hard to make a decision. This exercise should help you to find an interesting new restaurant to try. It will also let you practise describing and comparing similarities and differences.

Steps:

1 Go to google.com and search for interesting restaurants, within walking distance of your EF school. You might want to read reviews from a local newspaper's website or an online magazine.

2 Choose a restaurant that you would like to try and use mapquest.com to discover its exact location.

3 Type a short essay explaining why you chose this restaurant. Your essay should compare your restaurant to others that you found online or have already tried.

4 While you are reading about local restaurants on the internet, copy any new words into an MS Excel spreadsheet, then look up the word at dictionary.com. Copy at least two definitions to the right of each new word.

5 In class, discuss your choice of restaurant with another student.

Unit 2 Stages of life

There are many different ways for you to practise using future verb tenses. One good method is to think about your future and set new goals for yourself. As well as giving you practice in using future verb tenses, this iLab link will also help you to write summaries, set a life goal, and give you plenty of practice in reading English.

To begin the exercise, go to www.google.com and type: 'essay + old + stages in life' in the search window. This should give you a list of essays that discuss different life stages. Choose two essays from the list that interest you and read them both. When you have finished reading the essays, type up a summary of both of them.

Now, if you have time, have a think about what things you most want to do with your life. Type a short essay describing your most important life goal. Share your goal with your classmates.

Unit 3 Getting a deal

This exercise is intended to help you identify some of the world's best negotiators. As well as using negotiation vocabulary, this iLab link lets you practise 'make' and 'do' expressions and writing topic sentences.

Steps:

1 Use one of your favourite search engines, such as google.com, yahoo.com or dogpile.com, to find a negotiator from your home country, the USA and one other country of your choice.

2 Type up answers to the following questions: Who are some of the world's best negotiators? Are there differences in the way they argue? What different styles do they use?

3 Use your answers to write an essay about negotiation.

4 Next, rewrite your essay into a five-minute speech.

5 Present your speech to the class and be prepared to answer questions about the negotiators you chose.

Unit 4 Good for you!

Preventative health measures, such as a good diet and plenty of exercise, are important if you want to avoid frequent visits to the doctor. In this exercise, you will look at different ways to keep fit by reading about how professional athletes stay fit and healthy.

Use google.com or a website, such as bouldering.com, to find athletes from four different sports that interest you. Typing www.'sport of your choice'.com will usually give you lots of detail about a specific sport of interest to you. Discover what the different athletes do to keep themselves fit and healthy.

Copy all the important information you find out about each athlete into an MS Word document. Then, type out an essay describing what you learnt. You could also include information about yourself, such as: Do you play any sports? Why / Why not? Finally, read out your essay to other members of the class.

iLab links

Unit 5 Dealing with disaster

All around the world, accidents and disasters happen every day. Use the Internet to find an article from an English language online newspaper about a recent disaster or accident. Try to find something that happened in the city you are staying in or that you come from.

Steps:

1 Start by going to www.google.com and searching for an online newspaper.

2 Locate an interesting disaster or accident article and print it out.

3 Read through the article and write down any words that are new to you.

4 Look up the new words in a dictionary and take note of their meanings.

In class, summarise your article for your group, using the following headings as a guide:

a What happened?

b Who / What was involved?

c Where did it happen?

d Could the accident in your article have been prevented? If so, how?

e Have you experienced a similar accident?

Unit 6 Family values

Did you play games as a child? What games were the most popular? What games did you like best? This iLab link will take you back to your youth as you research a child's game from your own country. You will also practise summarising using sequence adverbs.

Steps:

1 Go to www.google.com and search for 'children's games + (name of your country)'.

2 Choose a game from your search list.

3 Answer the following questions:

  a What is the name of the game?

  b Where did the game originate from and when?

  c What, in your opinion, is the purpose of the game? (e.g., was it created for children to practise counting, rhyming words or vocabulary?)

Example:

Game: skipping rope / jump rope

Origin: location unknown, started around 1800's

Purpose: to practise counting

4 Describe the game in one or two paragraphs using sequencing adverbs, e.g. 'first', 'second', 'next', 'then', 'after that', 'in the end' and 'finally'.

5 In class, discuss any children's games you know of where a similar game is played in other cultures. For example, the British game of 'rock, scissors, paper' has Japanese and Korean versions, as well as a more difficult Arabic version.

Unit 7 Good behaviour

Every culture has its own set of taboos; that is, forbidden actions or behaviours. Interestingly, taboos in one culture often differ from those in another. In this iLab link, you will discover and research taboos from various cultures.

Steps:

1 Go to www.google.com and enter 'taboos' in the search field.

2 Make notes on two or three taboos from any site that you choose.

3 Use your notes to write an essay explaining the taboos you researched. How are they different from or similar to taboos in your culture?

4 Now, write a travellers' do / don't list for a country of your choice. Make your list into a travel poster and send it around the class.

Follow-up activity:

Write a taboo you know of on a piece of paper, but do not add your name. The teacher will collect the papers and give a different one to each student. In small groups, discuss your taboo and try to guess where it comes from.

Unit 8 Looking back, moving forward

How do you view retirement? Do you see it as a time to sit back and relax or an opportunity to be active and try as many new things as possible? In this iLab link, you will consider different idioms that can be used when discussing the subject of retirement.

Look at the list of idioms below:

- on a splurge
- change of scenery
- find one's feet
- pass the time

- to be on easy street
- fall on hard times
- make the best of (something)
- sit back

Steps:

1 Look up the meaning of each expression on the internet by typing in the expression + 'dictionary', or the expression + 'idiom'.

2 Write down each definition.

3 Write your own example sentence for each idiom, using the context of 'retirement'.

Example:

Idiom: Put all your eggs in one basket.

Definition: To put all your money into one place / one investment / one plan.

Sentence: The gambler lost all his retirement savings when he put all his eggs in one basket in his last losing game.

4 Once you have completed the task, discuss and compare your answers with your classmates'.

Page 6 Exercises A, B & C

Good afternoon, ladies and gentlemen, and welcome to The Well-Dressed Chef. I'm your host, James Olaf. Today, we are going to make one of my favourite desserts, oatmeal-raisin cookies. Before we start, let's make sure we have all of the ingredients we will need: 250 grammes of butter (that's about one cup); one cup of brown sugar; two eggs; one teaspoon of vanilla; two cups of flour; one teaspoon of baking soda; two teaspoons of cinnamon; one teaspoon of cloves; two cups of oats; two cups of raisins and two cups of chocolate chips. Did you get all that? That's 250 grammes, or one cup, of butter; one cup of brown sugar; two eggs; one teaspoon of vanilla; two cups of flour; one teaspoon of baking soda; two teaspoons of cinnamon; one teaspoon of cloves; two cups of oats; two cups of raisins and two cups of chocolate chips.

OK then, let's get to work. The first thing we need to do is pre-heat the oven to 180 degree Celsius. Next, in a large bowl, beat together the butter and the brown sugar until the mixture is smooth and creamy. After that, add the eggs and vanilla, and beat. Then, in another bowl, sift the flour, baking soda, cinnamon and cloves. Add this to the butter mixture, and mix. Mmm! It smells like my grandmother's kitchen! She was such a wonderful baker and made the best oatmeal-raisin cookies! Anyway, now, slowly stir in the oats, raisins and chocolate chips.

Now get out your baking sheets. Drop tablespoons of the cookie mixture onto the baking sheets. Leave some space around each bit of the mixture for the cookies to spread out. Bake them in the oven for ten to twelve minutes.

[short pause]

And, through the magic of television, here we have our perfectly baked cookies! They should be moist and chewy. I can't wait to try one ... Mmm, it's sweet and delicious.

And there you have it, Grandma's oatmeal-raisin cookies. Try them tonight! Until next time, enjoy!

Page 11 Exercises C, D & E

Host:	Good afternoon, ladies and gentlemen, and welcome to It's a Wonderful World. Today, on our show, we are talking with award-winning Mexican chef, Fernando Lopez. Fernando has just returned from a competition in Japan, where he won first prize. Congratulations, Fernando!
Fernando:	Thank you!
Host:	Fernando, you were in Japan for three months before the competition. What's it like there?
Fernando:	Well, in a word, it's amazing. Everything is much different from home in Mexico.
Host:	Well, you were there for a cooking competition. What's the food like in Japan?
Fernando:	It's so good! I especially liked the eel sushi. It's really delicious.
Host:	Mmm! What does eel taste like?
Fernando:	It tastes fresh. It's mild. It doesn't really taste like fish. With sushi, you have wasabi, a spicy paste that tastes like mustard, and pickled ginger, which is a bit sour.
Host:	That sounds great!
Fernando:	In general, I think the Japanese eat much more fish than Mexicans, even though we eat fish, too. Their food is also much less heavy. Mexican food is really fresh and absolutely delicious, but I have to admit, it's not as light. In general, it's much spicier too. But that's what we are famous for!
Host:	Well, the food's hot, and the weather is hot, right?
Fernando:	I guess so. The weather in Mexico really depends on where you are. Along the coast, it's hotter and more humid than in the centre. In the mountains, it's drier and a bit cooler. That's another difference between Mexico and Japan. Winter in Mexico is mild. The winters in Japan are quite a bit colder than in Mexico. They definitely have a lot more snow! The summers in Japan are not as hot as they are in Mexico.
Host:	What surprised you about Japan?

Fernando:	That's an interesting question. I'd have to say it's what I learned about the people. The people in Japan behave quite a bit more formally when they meet you. Mexicans, on the other hand, behave more casually. The Japanese appear more reserved and serious at first, while Mexicans often seem more outgoing, relaxed and fun-loving. For that reason, people sometimes think Mexicans are friendlier, but that's really not true, of course. The Japanese I met were a bit reserved at first, but they were much more fun-loving than I expected. They have what I would call a wild sense of humour. They are hard-working, but they really know how to enjoy themselves, too. Work hard, play hard. In that way, I guess they are similar to Mexicans!
Host:	They have a reputation for working a lot; that's true.
Fernando:	They work longer every day than most people in the world, I think.
Host:	What other impressions did you have of Japan?
Fernando:	It's such a beautiful and clean country. I was also impressed by the mixture of traditional and modern culture. On the one hand, you have these peaceful traditional gardens, and on the other hand, modern skyscrapers. And the high-speed bullet train! That was interesting!
Host:	Oh? Did you ride on the bullet train?
Fernando:	Yes, from Osaka to Tokyo. I took the Hikari train, which isn't the fastest, but it's still exciting. It stops a bit more frequently than the fastest train. So it is a little slower, but it's a lot cheaper. That's important because everything costs so much in Japan! Daily life is a bit less expensive in Mexico.
Host:	Well, that's all we have time for today. Thank you for your insights, Fernando. Join us next time when we talk with travel writer, Jack Reeves, who has just returned from …

Page 13 Exercise A

1   What sports do you like best?
2   What is your best friend like?
3   What's the weather like in England?
4   What does pizza taste like?
5   What do olives look like?
6   Are you from Korea?
7   Do you like chocolate?
8   Can I pay cash?
9   Which do you like better, football or baseball?
10 Which city do you prefer, New York or London?
11 Do you prefer Italian food or Chinese food?
12 Does this bus go to the museum or to the library?
13 Do you prefer paying by cash?
14 How do you like to pay?

Page 19 Exercise G

Patrick:	Hey, Judy! Happy belated birthday! Do you feel any different now you've turned 30?
Judy:	Well, I didn't feel like a different person when I woke up on my 30th birthday, but erm … it was … it was an important event, so I did have a party and celebrate.
Patrick:	Do you feel that you've finally grown up and that you have to behave like a responsible and mature adult?
Judy:	No, I don't feel any pressure at all. Most of my friends are older than me anyway, so I don't feel that old. Although, I do feel like I can relate to some of the issues that people talk about when they're in their 30s.
Patrick:	What kind of issues?
Judy:	Erm, I suppose things like there are more pressures to find a partner … or if you're going to have children … and the whole thing about the biological clock ticking away.
Patrick:	Yeah.
Judy:	You know – things like that.
Patrick:	Sure, but I don't think I really felt the same pressures when I was in my 30s – of course I'm a man, so it's different – and I'm in my 40s now.
Judy:	Only just!
Patrick:	But, when I was in my 30s, I felt like I was still in my 20s, you know? I felt I was sort of behind myself age-wise, and now that I'm in my 40s, I do feel older and that I'm taking on more responsibility … and yet sometimes I still feel like I'm in my teens. Then one of my kids says 'Daddy' and I remember how old I am. Do you feel your personality's changed since you were in your teens, say, or early 20s?
Judy:	Erm, I've probably become a lot more confident and a lot more self-assured and, in that sense…you know, when I look back and I think of myself in my early 20s, I can see that in certain respects I was very naive, but then at the time I thought I was very wise, so … I don't know, it's difficult to say …
Patrick:	I think I've become more adventurous. When I was in my 20s, I was a rather insecure and timid person, but now I'm getting on a bit and I think, you know, why not? Maybe that'll continue as I get older, and I'll have a wild time in my 60s and end up going round the world in a hot air balloon!
Judy:	That's funny. I think I've become less adventurous. But I'm more content. I think it may be because I did things on my own more when I was younger, and I was very independent, and now I think I've sort of taught myself to rely on other people more.
Patrick:	Mmm, and how do you see your older years? How do you see yourself in the future?
Judy:	Maturing … gracefully! Erm, going grey with dignity. I don't know really. I guess I'd like to be able to retire very soon!
Patrick:	Hold on! You've just turned thirty. If anyone here is retiring soon, it'll be me!

thirteen
thirteenth
thirty
thirtieth
thirties

fourteen
fourteenth
forty
fortieth
forties

fifteen
fifteenth
fifty
fiftieth
fifties

sixteen
sixteenth
sixty
sixtieth
sixties

seventeen
seventeenth
seventy
seventieth
seventies

eighteen
eighteenth
eighty
eightieth
eighties

nineteen
nineteenth
ninety
ninetieth
nineties

Page 35 Exercise D

So, why is it that some negotiators are better than others? Is it because they spend longer planning their strategy than average negotiators? Do they justify their arguments with a lot of reasons? Are they more aggressive? Are they generally better communicators? Why is it exactly? Well, we did some research which showed that there are various factors that help to make a negotiator better than average – and some that don't. Firstly, more time spent planning strategies before a negotiation doesn't make a better negotiator. But there are several other things that do affect the outcome of a negotiation.

For example, an average negotiator will only present his goals in terms of the present. He does not look into the future to set goals that can have future value for his organisation. A good negotiator, on the other hand, takes a long-term view of things. This helps him, or her, to be able to make a lot more suggestions in a negotiation than an average colleague.

A good negotiator will also consider twice the number of alternatives and is prepared to make compromises. So, whereas the average negotiator will present single goals, a good negotiator will present the goals with alternatives. This means the difference between saying 'We want 20%' and 'We are looking for 20% but will consider 15% if …' See the difference? If you are prepared to make compromises and to give the other side a range of options, you are more likely to reach a good deal.

Finally, it seems from the research that average negotiators try to persuade the other side by using a lot of arguments and giving lots of reasons for them. Good negotiators don't do this. They just repeat a limited number of reasons and review points they have already made during the negotiation. A good negotiator will keep checking that everyone has understood these points.

Page 37 Exercises A, B & E

1   television
2   ambition
3   assumption
4   cancellation
5   collision
6   condition
7   conversation
8   decision
9   demonstration
10 description
11 explosion
12 information
13 invasion
14 negotiation
15 occasion
16 presentation
17 profession
18 investigation

A: I'd like a hotel room. What do you have available?

B: I have a single room for $300 dollars a night.

A: Oh, that wouldn't work out. I need a double, and I can't spend that much. What if I booked for five nights? Could you offer a discount?

B: I'm afraid that wouldn't be possible. We don't have a double for five nights. Supposing you only stayed three nights? We could give you a discount then.

A: How much of a discount would you give us?

B: Let's see. If you stayed three nights, we could give you a 5% discount.

A: Hmm. What if we stayed for four nights? Would you have anything available?

B: Well, I can offer you a triple for four nights.

A: How much would that cost?

B: Well, I could give you a 10% discount if you booked a triple for four nights. That would bring the cost down to $270 a night.

A: OK, for that, will you include breakfast?

B: Hmm, no, I'm sorry. We wouldn't be able to do that for that price.

A: OK, supposing I paid $275 a night? Would you include breakfast then?

B: We can give you a continental breakfast, but only if you pay for it separately.

A: It's a deal.

B: Good.

Page 52 Exercise D

Maggie:	What conditions do you usually treat, Paul?
Paul:	I have a lot of success treating insomnia, headaches and arthritis, but I treat lots of other health problems, too.
Maggie:	When you see a new patient, what's the first thing you do?
Paul:	The first thing I do is talk with the patient. It's very important to get to know the patient.
Maggie:	What do you talk about?
Paul:	Well, first I just make small talk. You know, we talk about the weather, or I ask them what they've been doing. This makes them more comfortable, since sometimes they're nervous about seeing me. Also, it helps me see their mental and emotional condition. Of course, I also ask specific questions about their medical history like a regular doctor would do.
Maggie:	And after that, you put needles in them?
Paul:	Not right away! First, I take their pulse, and I take a good look at their tongue. I listen carefully to their breathing, too.

Page 53 Exercises E & F

1

Maggie:	What conditions do you usually treat, Paul?
Paul:	I have a lot of success treating insomnia, headaches and arthritis, but I treat lots of other health problems, too.
Maggie:	When you see a new patient, what's the first thing you do?
Paul:	The first thing I do is talk with the patient. It's very important to get to know the patient.
Maggie:	What do you talk about?
Paul:	Well, first I just make small talk. You know, we talk about the weather, or I ask them what they've been doing. This makes them more comfortable, since sometimes they're nervous about seeing me. Also, it helps me see their mental and emotional condition. Of course, I also ask specific questions about their medical history like a regular doctor would do.
Maggie:	And after that, you put needles in them?
Paul:	Not right away! First, I take their pulse, and I take a good look at their tongue. I listen carefully to their breathing, too.

2

Maggie:	But it's hard to think of it as medicine, John.
John:	OK, but it's definitely healing. My patients feel much better, and they sleep better. It also helps people with high blood pressure.
Maggie:	What kind do you use?
John:	It really depends on what my patients like. If they don't like it, it won't work very well. Classical is good for a lot of people, though. Usually it's better if it's soft, so hard rock doesn't work very well for most people.

3

Maggie: So, Harold, you use smells to treat people.

Harold: That's right, Maggie. It doesn't work for everything, of course, but it's great for depression, headaches and sinus infections, just to mention a few of the conditions I've had some success with.

Maggie: Good to know. I guess I wouldn't be opposed to trying it.

4

Maggie: Well, Helen, I've heard that it's great for stress.

Helen: Definitely. Most people I treat come to me because of stress. I also treat a lot of people who have arthritis. They're usually quite satisfied with the treatment.

Maggie: What's your usual procedure, Helen?

Helen: I start by putting on some soft music, and I put oil on my hands. I rub my hands together, so they're warm, and then I start with the neck and shoulders. Are you interested in trying it?

Page 59 Exercise I

exercise

medicine

physical

important

example

tradition

Page 59 Exercise J

addiction

enemy

interested

satisfied

allergy

natural

successful

arthritis

personal

surgery

depression

energy

infection

prevention

Page 67 Exercises F & G

Interviewer:	We're talking to Stuart Price of the Disaster Preparation Foundation. Stuart is here to tell us how best to prepare for an earthquake. Even if you live in an area where earthquakes are uncommon, you should still pay attention, as minor earthquakes can be dangerous, too. Stuart, let's start with preparations. What should householders do to get ready before an earthquake hits?
Stuart:	Well, this is a very important point. The first thing any concerned citizens should do before a quake is to educate themselves. The more you know, the better prepared you'll be, and the less likely you'll be to panic during an earthquake situation.
Interviewer:	Good advice there, everyone. Stuart, are there any items that people should keep in their homes in preparation for an earthquake?
Stuart:	Yes. Good items to keep include a torch, spare batteries, candles and matches, some spare cash, bottled water and protective clothing like raincoats and dust masks.
Interviewer:	Dust masks? What are they for?
Stuart:	Immediately after an earthquake, the air can be filled with dust and particles, making it hard to breathe while you are outside. A dust mask protects you and allows you to move freely around.
Interviewer:	OK. Let's hope it never happens, but if an earthquake does hit your area, what should you do to keep safe during the event?
Stuart:	This is a difficult question to answer because earthquakes are unpredictable and can affect buildings and structures in different ways. The first and most important thing to remember during an earthquake is to try not to panic. I know this is a tough one, since what most people want to do straight after they feel a quake or tremor is run outside. But really, the best thing to do is stay where you are, especially if you are inside. During a quake, things move and parts of buildings fall off. If you run out of your home, you may feel safer, but you are likely to be hit by falling bricks or other pieces of debris. Earthquakes, together with the foreshocks and aftershocks that come with them, can last for over an hour in some cases, so be prepared to stay where you are for as long as necessary.
Interviewer:	What should a person do if they get trapped inside their house?

Stuart:	Again, the important thing is not to panic. After the tremors have stopped, you may have to wait some time before rescuers can reach you. So you will need to keep up your strength. It sounds crazy, but while you are trapped, try to stay calm and think of something nice. Don't scream or move around too much as you could cause more damage. Stay still and shout for help every couple of minutes.
Interviewer:	What about people who aren't trapped? What should they do after it's safe to move?
Stuart:	It's important that they don't start moving things or digging until professional help arrives. I've seen quakes before where people have put themselves in real danger by digging for their families underneath unstable buildings. While you are waiting for the emergency services to arrive, you can help by moving people away from the disaster site and making a list of all the missing people.
Interviewer:	That's a difficult situation for anyone to experience. Stuart, what advice would you give to people who are worried about losing a family member?
Stuart:	I would say; have faith. Emergency services are expert at rescuing people from earthquake sites. The operation to dig people out from under buildings can go on for days or even weeks in some cases. We never rest until we've accounted for everyone.

Page 72 Exercises H & I

Person 1

It was horrible. I was just sitting on the beach when I saw this massive wave coming towards the shore. At first I thought, 'Wow, that's quite a big wave.' But then it just kept getting bigger and bigger and I knew I had to run. I looked for my husband, but I couldn't see him anywhere. Some of the tourists on the beach were just standing still, staring at the wave, so I shouted at them to get off the beach. I made it to the hotel and so did my husband. Most of the people in our group were OK, but I know that some people didn't make it. I wish I could have done more to get people off the beach, but really, we only had a couple of seconds to react. I'm glad that I ran.

Person 2

Oh, I'm used to them now. I've lived in Kansas all my life and you just adapt, you know? They are a part of life here. The worst one I experienced was in 1962. My father saw it spinning in the distance and came running into the yard. By the look on his face, I knew it was headed straight for us. Me and my mom and my brother got down into the shelter. My father tried to get some of the animals into the barn, but there wasn't time, so he jumped down the stairs after us and bolted the door of the shelter.

We could hear all the noise and disturbance outside and it was really frightening. I thought maybe it would take our house away. Then it all went quiet for a while and I knew we were in the eye of the storm—that's when the centre of the column passes right above you. The noise started again soon enough. It seemed to go on forever. My brother was crying, but I was quite excited.

When it was safe to go out, we got quite a shock. Half the roof had been blown off the house! Most of them aren't that bad though.

Person 3

I love my job. Most people think I'm totally crazy, but it's such an unique experience and I love to watch it. The last big one I saw was in Indonesia. Some volcanoes spit out mud and dirt, but this one was really special. After the explosion, red-hot lava poured down the edges of the mountain. I got as close as I could, which was about a mile from the top of the mountain. Most of my team got scared and drove to a safer place, but I really wanted to see the lava. It's amazingly beautiful, but very hot and dangerous, and it moves surprisingly fast. That's why most of the villages beneath Mount Vesuvius got buried by lava all those years ago.

My car was totally destroyed and I ended up having to run away from what was really a river of fire. The air was filled with smoke, so it was hard to breathe and quite frightening, but I still think it was one of the best experiences of my life. I took some wonderful video which made it onto TV. Most of us never get to see such a rare and amazing natural event.

Person 4

It was in Costa Rica some years ago. I was travelling with a group of friends and it had been raining most of the week, so the ground was really wet and muddy. We'd had to dig the car we were driving out of the mud a few times. It was when we were driving up a steep hillside in heavy rain that it happened. Suddenly the car started moving backwards and we realised that we'd been driving into a river of mud which was flowing down the hill. The flow was so strong that the car was pushed down the hill by it. It was like our car had suddenly become a boat which we had no control over!

Most of us had no experience of driving in this sort of situation, so we just panicked and screamed. Eventually, the car came to a stop in some trees, but it was filled with muddy water and we were trapped. I wanted to get out of the car, but there was nowhere to go. We stayed there until some local people came and helped us to safety. Some of the local villages were totally destroyed by the mud, but thank goodness, we were all OK.

Page 74 Exercise F

A category one hurricane has winds of between 74 to 95 miles per hour. Storm surge is four to five feet above normal. It causes minor damage to bushes, trees and mobile homes. Some examples of this category include Hurricane Lili of 2002 in Louisiana and Hurricane Gaston of 2004 along the South Carolina coast.

A category two hurricane has winds of between 96 to 110 miles per hour. Storm surge is generally six to eight feet above normal. Damage is serious, but not severe. For example, some trees may blow down and windows and doors may be damaged. Examples of this category include Hurricane Frances of 2004, Florida and Hurricane Isabel of 2003 in North Carolina.

A category three hurricane has winds of between 111 to 130 miles per hour. Storm surge is around nine to twelve feet above normal and evacuation of coastal areas may be mandatory. Damage during a category three hurricane is severe. Coastal flooding may destroy small buildings and large homes can be damaged by flying objects. Examples include Hurricanes Jeanne, which hit Florida, and Ivan, which hit Alabama, both in 2004. Hurricane Katrina of 2005 struck New Orleans as a category three hurricane.

A category four hurricane has winds of between 131 to 155 miles per hour. Storm surge is generally 13 to 18 feet above normal. Evacuation of areas up to seven miles inland may be mandatory. Damage is extensive and extreme. For example, houses may have their roof blown off and buildings near the shore may collapse. Examples include Hurricane Charlie of 2004, which made landfall in Florida with winds of 150 mph. Hurricane Dennis of 2005 hit Cuba as a category four hurricane. Hurricane Wilma of 2005 struck Mexico as a category four hurricane.

A category five hurricane is the strongest type of hurricane. It has winds greater than 155 miles per hour. Storm surge is greater than 18 feet above normal. These storms cause catastrophic damage. Roofs on many buildings are completely destroyed, structural damage is common, and entire buildings may collapse or be blown away. Mobile homes are completely destroyed. All shrubs, trees and signs are blown down. Recent category five hurricanes include Hurricanes Mitch of 1998 and Isabel of 2003. Category five hurricanes that have made landfall include Camille of 1969 in Mississippi and Hurricane Andrew of 1992, which made landfall over Florida, causing massive damage and almost total destruction of some neighbourhoods.

Audio scripts

Unit 6

Page 83 Exercise F

Dad:	I'm all ears. What can I help you with?
Daniel:	Umm, I have to ask you questions about when you were my age. Mr Flores thinks that writing an essay about how our parents used to live is a good idea. He thinks it will make us appreciate how lucky we really are.
Dad:	Oh really? In that case, ask me anything you like.
Daniel:	OK. So tell me. How did it use to be?
Dad:	Well first of all, when I was your age I never used to speak to my dad like you speak to me. I used to have respect for my father. Yes, things used to be very different. We used to watch television. We used to listen to Walkmans. I used to have hair. Today, we stare at computers, listen to digital music and I save lots of money on haircuts and shampoo. But seriously, even family values have changed. Families used to spend more time together. They took vacations together. They watched TV together. They ate meals together. In my family, we used to eat dinner together every night. We talked about how our day was, what we learned in school and things like that. My dad, your granddad, told us about his day and job, too. The roles of mothers in families have changed quite a bit as well. Many mothers used to stay at home. They didn't use to work as much as they do now. Nowadays, many women work full time as well as take care of their families. In this day and age, with all the two-career couples and families, fathers aren't just working any more. They share in a lot of the housework, too.

Page 83 Exercise G

Dad:	We didn't use to have all the things you do now to entertain us, either. We needed to find other things to amuse ourselves with.
Daniel:	What things did you use to play with?
Dad:	We used to play with our friends outside, for example. Today, most kids are literally plugged into something somewhere indoors. Going to the cinema used to be considered going out. Now we have DVDs. And let's not forget what happened to music.
Daniel:	What?
Dad:	Well, it actually used to be music. Not the noise you kids listen to today.
Daniel:	Yeah? I'll bet Grandpa used to tell you the same thing.
Dad:	Actually, now that I think about it, he also used to complain about how family values were changing. He said that we had no idea what it was to earn money or appreciate the value of a dollar. In his day, he had to help support his family. He did lots of chores around the house and helped to take care of his brothers and sisters. And if he wanted pocket-money, he had to work at a job after school. He used to say that, when he was my age, Walkmans were radios and televisions were called books. He also used to tell me that I spent too much time in front of the TV screen.
Daniel:	Like you tell me about the computer screen.
Dad:	Yeah. I suppose you're right. I guess some things never change.

Page 85 Exercise G

'Used to' is usually pronounced 'used to'.

They used to travel all the time.
I used to like ice-cream.

The final '-ed' of the simple past of regular verbs can be pronounced in different ways.

After voiceless sounds, the final '-ed' is pronounced / t /.

mixed / worked / liked / kissed / promised
pushed / touched / asked / stopped / finished

After voiced sounds, the final '-ed' is pronounced / d /.

used / planned / smiled / loved / sneezed
pleased / dreamed / closed / arrived

After / t / and / d /, the final ' ed' is pronounced / id /.

wanted / waited / needed / counted
dated / avoided / hated / traded

Page 85 Exercise H

cleaned / cooked / decided / heated / invited
lifted / listened / lived / pulled / shopped
talked / thanked / tried / visited / watched

Page 85 Exercise I

1   Denise mixed the ingredients in a bowl.
2   Max used the last light bulb.
3   Jeffrey hated golf, so he played tennis instead.
4   The baby kissed his mother and smiled.
5   William watched videos and listened to music at the same time.
6   The little boy pulled and pushed his train around the room.
7   I really needed that vacation.
8   Sal and Sid finally decided to get married.
9   Marina stopped eating cake and started eating fruit.
10 She was pleased that she dreamed about him.

Page 88 Exercise C

1   ten
2   mice
3   fiddle
4   moon
5   farmer
6   cut

Page 89 Exercise E

1   fight
2   stock
3   loose
4   say
5   table
6   hold
7   lose
8   yawning
9   pass
10 sup

Page 91 Exercise H

Interviewer:	Thank you for letting us join you for breakfast this morning.
Jason:	It's our pleasure. Right, Nick?
Nick:	Right.
Interviewer:	How old are you, Nicholas?
Nick:	I'm eight.
Jason:	He'll be nine next month.
Interviewer:	Wow. That's great! What do you want for your birthday?
Nick:	My dad's already bought tickets to a baseball game. We're going together.
Interviewer:	That sounds like fun. I'll bet you and your dad do a lot of things together.
Nick:	No ... well, sometimes he's pretty busy.
Jason:	Yeah. But we try to spend as much time as we can together. Don't we, Nick?
Nick:	Yeah. This afternoon we're going to the park.
Interviewer:	What's it like being a single dad?
Jason:	It's wonderful. It's difficult. It's really great most of the time. I guess my biggest problem is time. There aren't enough hours in the day.
Interviewer:	Tell me about a typical day. How does your day start?
Jason:	Well, we get up at about 6.30. I have to be at work by 8.30. School starts at 9.00.
Interviewer:	Who makes breakfast?
Nick:	Dad usually makes toast. I get the cereal. We always have breakfast together.
Jason:	It's our time to talk. I don't get home from the office until after 7.00 some nights. Then there's only time for a quick dinner, homework, bath ... Nick has to be in bed by 9 o'clock. That's when I do the laundry and stuff like that.
Nick:	I do laundry sometimes.
Interviewer:	Really?
Jason:	That's right. He does. He helps out around here a lot.
Interviewer:	You said that you sometimes don't get home until after 7.00. What does Nicholas do after school?
Jason:	He usually goes to the park and plays with his friends for a while. And then he comes home.
Nick:	We keep the key in a secret hiding place. It's under the flowerpot. Oh, I guess I shouldn't have told you that.
Interviewer:	I won't tell. I promise. How does it feel to be home alone, Nick? Do you ever feel lonely or afraid?
Nick:	Well... sometimes. But then I call my dad. I can call him any time I want.
Jason:	Yeah. He's got all the numbers: my pager, the cell phone. I'm never more than a phone call away if he needs me.
Interviewer:	So, Nick, what do you do until your dad gets home from work?
Nick:	I watch TV, or I play computer games. Sometimes I get dinner ready.
Interviewer:	You can cook?
Jason:	He can do simple things. His specialty is peanut butter and jelly. Right, Nick?
Nick:	Yeah. I guess mostly Dad cooks.
Jason:	We eat a lot of frozen dinners. I'm not a great cook.
Interviewer:	May I ask how long you've been a single father?
Jason:	My wife and I divorced when Nick was only a year old. She had ... well, let's just say she had problems. Nick's grandmother wanted to take him, but I said no. I wanted to raise my son. And that's how it's turned out.
Interviewer:	Nick, you must miss having a mum.
Nick:	Sometimes. But I have Dad.
Interviewer:	You love him a lot, don't you?
Nick:	Yeah. I'm very lucky he's my dad.
Interviewer:	Seems like you're pretty lucky, too, Jason. Nick's a great kid.
Jason:	He's the best. I don't know what I'd do without him.

Page 100 Exercises E & F

Marla: Welcome again to the 'Mind Your Manners' radio show. I'm Marla Stewart, and I'm ready to listen and help you with all your questions about proper manners. Today, we are talking to Harvey. Harvey is throwing his first dinner party and has a few queries about what a good host is expected to do. Good morning, Harvey. How can I help you today?

Harvey: Good morning, Marla. And thanks for talking to me. Actually, I think I have pretty good manners. My parents were careful to teach me how important they can be. So I guess I know the basics.

Marla: What do you mean, the basics?

Harvey: You know, things like, it's rude to put your elbows on the table, it's impolite to speak with your mouth full and it's definitely wrong to burp.

Marla: That's true. So what do you need help with?

Harvey: Well, there are a few things I'm not sure about. For example, what should I do when I make a toast?

Marla: Good question! Just remember, it's important to make the toast sincere. And when you clink glasses, it is essential to look the other person in the eye.

Harvey: Hmm. What about talking to the guests? There will be quite a few people and I don't want anyone to feel uncomfortable or left out.

Marla: You're right. It's your job to make your guests as comfortable as possible. Be prepared to introduce people. Most people are hesitant to introduce themselves. Also, be sure to seat people with common interests next to each other. This way you'll be free to enjoy your party more. And if that isn't enough, don't be afraid to ask a friend for help.

Harvey: Those are good suggestions. But I have one more question. What do you do when your guests stay too long?

Marla: Ah, yes. This is a common problem. It's difficult to tell your guests that they've overstayed their welcome. You don't wanna to hurt their feelings. I suggest you give them hints. You might say something like, 'Oh my, look at the time.' Or, 'I've got to wake up early tomorrow.' And if that doesn't work, offer them another cup of coffee. By the third time, they should understand that it's time to go. And speaking of going, it's time for us to go to a commercial break. So stay tuned. We'll be right back after these messages.

Audio scripts

Unit 8

Page 120 Exercises A & B

Sonia: Hi, Guys! I've decided to start working.

JP: But you're only 14! What kind of job are you going to look for? Whatever it is, you'll begin at a very low position because of your age.

Sonia: Thanks very much, JP! I wish you could be a bit more supportive.

Mariela: Actually, Sonia, if I were you, I'd wait until you're 18, because then you'll be paid more. And maybe you could get a job at one of those fancy department stores selling cool designer clothes and getting discounts just because you work there.

Sonia: But, Mariela, that means I have to wait four more years to start working! I know I'm only 14, but I saw a 'Help Wanted' sign at Super Burger.

JP: You must be crazy! Working at a fast food restaurant? At Super Burger! If you work there, you'll never leave. That's what happens to everyone that works in places like Super Burger. They stay there until they're old and fat.

Mariela: JP! That's not true. Plenty of people work at Super Burger for a while and then move on to other jobs. What about you, Mark? Weren't you thinking about getting a job, too?

Mark: Well, I think working at Super Burger might be good for you, Sonia, but I'm not going to work for anyone. I'm going to be my own boss. In fact, I've also been thinking about starting my own business, delivering packages and newspapers door to door.

Mariela: My father says international business is where the money is. When I start work, it'll be at an international company where I'll meet people from all over the world. Since travelling is what I like best, I'll look for a job in a company where they'll ask me to travel all over.

Sonia: Yeah, that'll be great for you, Mariela, but you can afford to wait until you leave school before you start working. I want the experience and some money now. I'm not saying I'm going to work at Super Burger all my life, but I have to start somewhere. My father used to wash dishes before he actually bought his own restaurant. All I'm saying is that you have to begin doing something.

JP: Well that's true. And your father's very successful now, Sonia. When did he start working?

Sonia: I think he said that he started when he was 15.

Mark: I don't want to discourage you, Sonia, but what do you know about working at Super Burger? Except that you like the food, that is.

Mariela: Well, there! She's the perfect candidate for the job. She likes the food!

Sonia: Why not? If I like it, I'll be happy to sell it and even happier to prepare it.

JP: Guys, I guess she's made her decision. We'll just have to support her.

Mark: Hey, does that mean we can get free food from you?

Mariela: OK. I'd recommend not going to eat where Sonia's gonna work. She might get into trouble. You don't want her to get fired from her first job, do you?

JP, Mariela: Good luck, Sonia!

Page 121 Exercise A

1 What's their new house like?
2 What do they look like?
3 What does it feel like?
4 Who does he like?
5 Who do you agree with?
6 What's wrong with Maggie?
7 Why didn't they buy the car?
8 What do you do?
9 What did you use to do?
10 Do you think they're lucky?

Page 122 Exercise D

1 shouted
2 called
3 yelled
4 played
5 walked
6 nodded
7 showed
8 loaded
9 knocked
10 started

Page 122 Exercise H

black
shed
block
pick
a
foot
cup
we
far
shoe
fur
play
five
now
toy
near
rare

Intermediate English **3**
(CEF version) B1

Signum International
S.a.r.l. Luxembourg, Zug Branch
Zeughausgasse 9a
6301 Zug
Switzerland

© Signum International
S.à.r.l. Luxembourg,
Zug Branch, Zug, 2009

First published 2009
This impression (lowest digit)
  5 7 9 10 8 6 4
ISBN 978-3-03758-073-8

Acknowledgements
EF Education First would like to thank the many teachers, academic directors, and language experts who have participated in the development of EF's library of educational materials. Beata Schmid, Ph.D. and the faculty members of EF schools worldwide have contributed to the continual development, implementation, assessment and revision of this series. The following EF International Language Schools (ILS) faculty members and writers created material for the 3rd Edition of EF's Efekta™ System General English textbook series.

Cheryl Albright (ILS Seattle)
Ludmila Andersson (ILS Brisbane)
Laurie Barlow (ILS Vancouver)
Rena Bartlett (ILS Boston)
Sophie Behagg (ILS Brighton)
Jason Berry (ILS Boston)
Jamie Collinson (ILS London)
Ian Devey (ILS Bournemouth)
Kirsty Dickson (ILS Vancouver)
Sandy Dzogan (ILS Toronto)
Thomas Engfer (ILS Los Angeles)
Sarah Finck (ILS Boston)
Damian Flores (ILS Miami)
Monica Guerrero (ILS Miami)

Lisa Guglielmi (ILS Vancouver)
Neil Hammond (ILS Vancouver)
Grant Hitchcock (ILS Brighton)
Ted Kelsey (ILS New York)
Leslie Lloyd (ILS Santa Barbara)
Luca Marchiori (ILS Bournemouth)
Kristy McKee (ILS Santa Barbara)
Corinne Meers (ILS Sydney)
Hans Mol (SCC Australia)
Kim Nowitsky (ILS Vancouver)
Samantha Palfrey (ILS Toronto)
Vaughan Thomas
Carol Uy (ILS Toronto)
Elise Guillen (ILS Vancouver)

Design:	Masterpress (Hong Kong) Ltd.
Printing:	Masterpress (Hong Kong) Ltd.
Photography:	Getty Images
Audio Production:	Southern Cross Connexxions / Fracas, Australia
Development Editors:	Jane Lee, Luca Marchiori, Celia Wigley
Level Editors:	Kirsten Campbell-Howes, Aelred Doyle, Erika Fässler-Nelson, Luca Marchiori, Hans Mol
Publisher:	Jane Lee
Editorial Director:	Christopher McCormick, Ph.D.

Printed in Hong Kong